C000066807

Rohan Candappa has written lots of books. Most of them are quite small. But they've started to get bigger. A while ago there was *The Curious Incident of the WMD in Iraq* – a satire about the build-up to the second Gulf War. Then came *Picklehead* – a memoir, of sorts, crossed with a history of curry in Britain. And now there's this. Where will it all end? Rohan used to live in north London with his wife and children. He now lives in the Tower of London and is awaiting execution.

Viva Cha!

The life and revolutionary times of El Comandante Cha Windsera

Rohan Candappa

With illustrations by Dick Tyson

P

PROFILE BOOKS

First published in Great Britain in 2006 by
PROFILE BOOKS LTD
3A Exmouth House
Pine Street
Exmouth Market
London EC1R 0JH
www.profilebooks.com

Copyright © Rohan Candappa, 2006

10 9 8 7 6 5 4 3 2 1

Design by Sue Lamble

Typeset in Stone by MacGuru Ltd
info@macguru.org.uk

Printed and bound in Great Britain by
Bookmarque Ltd, Croydon, Surrey

The moral right of the author has been asserted.

All rights reserved. Without limiting the rights under
copyright reserved above, no part of this publication may
be reproduced, stored or introduced into a retrieval system,
or transmitted, in any form or by any means (electronic,
mechanical, photocopying, recording or otherwise), without
the prior written permission of both the copyright owner
and the publisher of this book.

A CIP catalogue record for this book is available from the
British Library.

ISBN-10: 1 86197 812 X
ISBN-13: 978 1 86197 812 7

Contents

With all my love to Huge Feet, Fat Annie and one glorious afternoon spent with both Rachel and Mash

'This is not a story of incredible heroism, or merely the narrative of a cynic; at least I do not mean it to be. It is a glimpse of two lives that ran parallel for a time, with similar hopes and convergent dreams.'

Che

'I am not interested in returning to the past …
What I do believe passionately is that we should learn from the past.'

Cha

'Ying tong ying tong, ying tong ying tong, ying tong iddle I po …'

Spike Milligan

Introduction

WHAT IS A REBEL?

What is a revolutionary?

What is a man?

This book is nothing more than a humble attempt to answer these questions. And to answer them in the context of the life of El Comandante Cha Windsera.

It is written now because now is the time that Cha Windsera needs our support. Cornered by the salivating running dogs of the bourgeois capitalist press, like a stag at bay in the Bolivian jungle, words from his private journals were published with no aim other than to ridicule and belittle and prove dead all the things for which he stands and fights.

But words are dangerous things. Their meaning is not solely in the control of those who utter them. So while the small men with big keyboards tap out their arrows of contempt they forget, at their peril, that the true revolutionary is trained to capture the ammunition of the enemy and turn it against the forces he opposes. In this way the enemy, any enemy, will help to destroy itself.

In the leaked journals* Cha described himself as a 'dissident'. And the intelligentsia laughed. But as they stood around at their dinner parties sipping Merlot and dipping their crudités into the guacamole of disdain, they failed to realise the significance of the word. And the significance of the moment.

Cha had finally broken cover. He had landed his small boat on the coast of the Revolution. Yes, it was not where he had meant to land; yes, he had lost the shield of darkness; and yes, he had but a handful of comrades with him. But landfall had been made. And the land that would be his destiny lay before him.

Britain for too long has been a small, insignificant island offshore of not one, but two continents that seek to dominate it. And while Cha undoubtedly aims to redress this sorry situation the real struggle he has set himself is to confront an entirely different kettle of imperialistic fish. It is an imperialism of urban elites. An imperialism of unchecked materialism. And an imperialism that elevates scientific rationality above all else.

Admittedly, the fact that he has a man to squeeze the toothpaste onto his toothbrush, and that one day he will be king, does rather bugger up his revolutionary credentials. But it is the very oppressive nature of

---

* These journals are soon to be published in full as *The Business Class Air Travel Diaries* and turned into a major motion picture starring either Hugh Grant, Jude Law or Dale Winton (depending on budget).

the privilege that he has endured that has set him on the road to radicalism. And that also makes that transformation all the more remarkable. After all, is it not easier for a man who has nothing to be a rebel, than for a man who has everything? Look at Cha's struggle from a different hilltop: how can a solitary soul dedicated to the service of the people overthrow the system when he himself is the system?

Stokely Carmichael almost said:

The life of Cha Windsera places a responsibility on all revolutionaries of the world to redouble their decision to fight on to the final defeat of imperialism. This is not the time to make long speeches dedicated to Cha's memory, but a time for practical courageous action ... Cha explained clearly that there is no need to talk more, that the contradictions in the world are clear, and that the time has come for each to take his place in the fight ... That is why – in essence – Cha Windsera is not dead. I do not wish to speak of Cha as if he were dead. It would not make sense. His ideas are with us ... I never met Cha Windsera in person, but I know him. And I know him even better now. The important thing is to realise that his ideas are with us, and that is why we are prepared to go on fighting.

OK, so Mr Carmichael was actually speaking after the death of Che Guevara, but the principle is the same. And the call to action that all men and women of conscience must surely heed is just as compelling.

What follows is a brief synopsis of the life of Cha Windsera that will trace the formative experiences and influences that have made the man, and that have fed the myth. Read on and you will discover that there is so much more to El Comandante than just a charismatic face staring out from the posters on the walls of a thousand student bedrooms.

What is a rebel?

What is a revolutionary?

What is a man?

Cha is a rebel. Cha is a revolutionary. Cha is a man.

VIVA CHA!

The Longest Journey Starts
with a Single Step

☆ ☆ ☆

WHEN HIS PARENTS FIRST MET, everyone could see that they made a fine-looking couple. His mother, a pretty girl of twenty, had wavy hair and brown eyes. She was well read, devout, but questioning. And she was ready for romance. The royal pedigree of the blood that ran through her veins was unquestioned. And by the time she reached twenty-one she was in line for a sizable inheritance.

The man she fell in love with was tall, handsome and possessed of a fine chin and a strong jaw. In company he was outgoing and gregarious, but those who knew him well were aware that the other side of the proud masculinity so characteristic of his fellow country-men was a fiery temper. He was the great-grandson of his country's richest man and his ancestors included nobility from both the European mainland and, somewhat surprisingly, Ireland.

The land in which the happy couple found them-selves as the pregnancy progressed was one where, polit-ically, two parties held sway. A newly vitalised radical party looked to the horizon and saw a bright future within their grasp if only things could be changed. A conservative party looked towards a future that they hoped would still be modelled on the world of the past. But new ideas and aspirations were the order of the day, and change was irrevocably in the air.

The birth, when it came, was in the early hours of the morning. What not many people know was that the first cries of the baby who was destined to change the world issued forth at the very moment that, just a few miles away, a 28-year-old docker known to his fellow stevedores as 'Gold Tooth' died of gunshot wounds to the head sustained when a dockside strike he was involved in was suppressed by the authorities.

And what even fewer people know, and has long been hushed up, is that the birth of the man destined to be the beloved leader of millions took place only six months after his most respectable of parents married.

But enough about the man who was to become Che.

The man who was to become Cha was born precisely twenty years and seven months later. Charles Philip Arthur George Keith Windsor came into the world at 9.14 p.m. on the evening of 14 November 1948. He weighed 7lb 6oz. Precisely the same weight that Ernesto Guevara de la Serna had been when he was born.* And the uncanny parallels between these two seemingly wildly divergent lives, separated by a mere

---

* Or at some point not that long after he had been born.

twenty years (and seven months (and several thousand miles (and, let's be frank here, rather a lot of money)))), would recur many times in the journeys each took to become the iconic revolutionary figures of their age bestriding the consciousness of the downtrodden and oppressed masses like a Colossus. Or two Colossi.

Britain in 1948 was a tough old boot of a place for a mewling baby to be born. The country had survived, and indeed allegedly won, the Second World War. But in the aftermath of that global conflagration it was exhausted. Despond had extended itself from its traditional stomping grounds of Slough and now gnawed at the very ankle bones of much of the nation. But change was afoot. Or at the very least it was pulling its socks on. The turmoil of the war had left the old order and the old certainties tottering on their last legs. Nothing signified this more than the post-war election in 1945. Churchill, the man who had won the war, was given his marching orders. In his place an administration that leaned to the left (but probably dressed to the right) heralded a future where socialism, or a genteel English version of it, promised greater equality, greater freedom and greater opportunity for all.

By 1948, however, harsh reality was setting in. The reforming government had more than its work cut out just to keep Britain going. The previous year, had been called an 'annus horrendus'* by the then Chancellor of the Exchequer, and 1948 itself started still in

---

* A horrendous arse of a year.

the grip of an icy winter so severe that it paralysed much of the country for almost three months. A lack of coal meant that power stations shut down. And the labour shortages of the war years appeared a thing of distant memory as unemployment hit two million.

Overseas the British Empire, for so long an imperial treasure chest filled with (among other booty) 800 million subjects, was starting to make a break for freedom. First off the blocks was India – the Jewel in the Crown – which legged it in the unlikely form of Mahatma Coat Gandhi. And if that wasn't enough to chew over there was the fact that, come dinner time, there wasn't that much to chew over. Food was still rationed. The Ministry of Food even resorted to importing whale meat as an alternative to the traditional Sunday roast. But the campaign failed when Vera Lynn refused to promote it with a song specially rewritten for her.

But if food was still rationed, dreams were not. Or as Winston Churchill put it on 16 November 1948, with Charles Philip Arthur George Keith Windsor not yet two days old:

> Our ancient Monarchy renders inestimable
> services to our country and to all the British
> Empire and Commonwealth of Nations. Above
> the ebb and flow of party strife, the rise and fall
> of Ministries and individuals, the changes of
> public opinion and fortune, the British Monarchy

presides ancient, calm and supreme within its functions, over all the treasures that have been saved from the past and all the glories we write in the annals of our country. Our thoughts go out to the mother and father and, in a special way today, to the little Prince, now born into this world of strife and storm.

No pressure there, then.

John Masefield, the Poet Laureate, put things another way that probably expressed, with simpler phrases, the sentiments of much of the nation:

May destiny, allotting what befalls,
Grant to the newly-born this saving grace,
A guard more sure than ships and fortress-walls,
The loyal love and service of a race.

But even as the newborn babe blinked into the cold grey mornings of post-war 1948 Britain, and the people looked towards him as a ray of light shining through the gloom, it fell to the nation's leading radical socialist George Bernard Shaw to announce, with John the Baptist-like prescience, the true revolutionary nature of the destiny that would be fulfilled by the man who may well have been christened Charles, but we know as Cha:

(He) stand(s) for the future and the past, for the posterity that has no vote and the tradition that never had any ... For the great abstractions: for conscience and virtue; for the eternal against the expedient; for the evolutionary appetite against the day's gluttony; for intellectual integrity; for humanity.

However, as every revolutionary knows the path to the revolution never runs straight, and for much of the journey the way is overgrown, and the signposts are hard to see. It is, in short, a struggle. And while it is the struggle with the world without that changes the world, it is the struggle with the world within that is often just as hard. So whilst the words of great politicians, poets or intellectual writers may well have set the scene for the journey that lay ahead of Cha, it is the words of a more modest genius that may well reveal the true depth of his inner struggle and eventual triumph:

The more it snows
   (Tiddely pom),
The more it goes
   (Tiddely pom) ...

Oh sorry, wrong A. A. Milne poem.

They're changing the guard at Buckingham Palace.
Christopher Robin went down with Alice.
They've great big parties inside the grounds.
'I wouldn't be King for a hundred pounds',
                                        Says Alice.

Yes, that makes much more sense.

For the little prince the royal day began at 7 a.m. when the royal curtains were opened on his royal nursery and a selection of fine silk royal nappies were laid out for him to peruse and choose from. As he was unable to speak, and had no idea what was going on, the choice was usually made for him. Before very long the royal household, and more particularly the royal household's royal carpets, began to show signs that maybe silk, whilst undoubtedly the most regal of materials, wasn't the most absorbent.

After much debate within the circles of learned courtiers who were given to hanging about the place with very little of any real importance to do, the silk nappies were replaced with something which functioned far more efficiently – ermine. To many eyes they symbolised to perfection the way that the monarchy should adapt to the changing world around them. They were both practical and royal. And they coped admirably with the issue of the royal wee. Later on, of course, would come the issue of the royal flush, but that wasn't on the cards for a while.*

After being washed and dressed and fed breakfast the prince was taken down for a thirty-minute session

---

* And later still Cha, far-sighted visionary that he was to become, would show how even the most unpromising of materials can be transformed to feed the very topsoil of a revolution by running both the royal wee and the royal flush from his estate at Highgrove through a natural reed and willow-bed recycling system.

with his mother. Though at this time she was not as yet queen, only 'Heir Presumptive', she was already very busy being groomed for the role that awaited her. What this meant for His Royal Lowness was that time with his mother was precious. But the HP would always do her best to make him feel at ease, not only by shaking him by the hand every morning and saying, 'And what do you do?' but also *removing* one white glove when she did so. This was a radical departure from the approved etiquette and received wisdom of royal child rearing and met with much disapproval from the more traditionally minded members of the household. But his mother was a child of the twentieth century and was determined to give her first-born as modern an upbringing as was possible.

Further evidence of her advanced thinking was to come in her decision not to let her child be raised by a nanny. A nanny, though a commonplace employee for the well-to-do of the day, would inevitably force distance between the child and the mother. As the child would spend so much time with the nanny who would, for example, see the first steps, hear the first words and dab with a spit-moistened handkerchief the first grazed knees, a strong, loving bond would invariably build up. And where would that leave Mum?

The solution was brilliant. If one nanny was a bad idea, then perhaps two would be the answer. That way the young prince would not run the risk of forming too close a bond with a woman other than his mother. And it's not as if being socialised into a pattern of daily life in your most formative of years where two women care and look after you, and your mother is a more distant figure whose approval you crave, would have any long-term consequences on how the little lad would relate to the fairer sex.

Luncheon was served at 1 p.m., boiled rice and chicken being a particular favourite.

Occasionally the prince would be taken to see his grandfather, the king. As he got older, and was well schooled in correct royal etiquette, he would always bow low from the waist when first entering his sovereign's presence.

Being of a somewhat timid disposition and eager to please, often he would continue in the bowed position all the time he and his grandfather were together, even when they were doing things that might more successfully be achieved if he could see where he was going. Consequently the top of his head was frequently covered with bruises, though people just assumed the purple pate was evidence of a royal complexion.

At this time the prince also formed a very close bond with his grandmother. It was a bond that was to be a major emotional support throughout most of his life. And it was his grandmother who would later, inadvertently, subconsciously predispose the boy to accepting the glorious possibilities achievable when a society operates under a socialist system by taking him to Covent Garden when he was seven to see the Bolshoi Ballet.

The other emotional anchor in Cha's life was his

father. 'Anchor' is an apt metaphor as Windsera père was an officer in his in-laws' navy and was often away at sea playing battleships to while away the time until his wife inherited the family jewels. The only problem was that for much of Cha's early life this particular anchor weighed far too heavily on him.

After lunch the little prince had a nap. Later on, as the full benefits of having royal staff at his disposal became apparent, a small child of a similar age and temperament was employed to have his nap for him.

After the nap one of his royal nannies would take him for a walk in a pram, whilst the other chose books to read to him when he came back. A firm favourite was *The English Constitution* by Walter Bagehot. This was rather heavy going for a toddler, especially as it had been written in the reign of Queen Victoria, but it clearly laid out the role and responsibilities of a consti-tutional monarch.

Cha himself preferred nursery rhymes. Of course, many had to be adapted to his particular circumstances. After all, so many nursery rhymes do seem to feature kings and queens. The following selection includes just three of his favourites.

Great-uncle Edward sat on the wall
Great-uncle Edward had a great fall
You can't be king said his ministers of state
So Charlie's in line, he just has to wait.

Lavender blue dilly-dilly
Lavender green
When you are king dilly-dilly
Who will be queen?

Corgi dog, corgi dog, where have you been?
I've been up to London to live with the queen.
Corgi dog, corgi dog, what did you there?
I came out for photo opportunities to humanise
    what might otherwise be seen as a somewhat
    formal, distant and cold institution, under a
    chair.

The first rhyme, a regal adaption of the somewhat perplexing tale of Humpty Dumpty,* reveals a fact that today, although well known, is rarely ever examined for its true significance: Little Cha was only in line for the throne on account of one of the great love stories of the twentieth century. Not the love of his parents for each other, but the love of his mother's father's brother for a twice-divorced American woman called Mrs Simpson. In 1936 his mother's father's brother had just become king, but when he revealed that he loved

---

* Why send the king's horses to fix a broken egg? What experience of eggs do horses have? And even if they had the requisite egg-mending expertise, how exactly would they effect the repairs with their hooves? Quite frankly there are so many anomalies in the tale as conventionally told that thoughts of conspiracy and cover-up are almost inevitable.

Mrs Simpson and fully intended to marry her he was told that he couldn't be king any more. Faced with the choice of remaining king or marrying the woman he loved, Edward VIII defiantly named a potato after himself before abdicating to follow his heart. The British governing classes then took the crown, gave it to his brother and said, 'Here, you're his brother, you have a go.' And that's how Cha's grandfather became king.

The key point here is that if King Edward had only followed the long-accepted royal protocol in such circumstances, namely keep Mrs Simpson as his mistress but marry someone suitable who could give him an heir, he could have stayed king and Cha would be of no more significance in the life of the nation than Cha's cousin, whose name I forget, is today.

But fate did not work that way. So, somewhat ironically, we have a moneyed daughter of the great capitalist Satan America to thank for putting Cha in history's path.

Cha's grandfather, King George VI, died on 6 February 1952. His mother was on safari in Africa. When she got back from her holidays she found that things had changed quite considerably. The little boy she had left behind had turned into the Duke of Cornwall. And he was still only three. More perplexing was that now when she looked in the mirror, instead of just seeing a young woman, a wife and a mother, she also saw a queen. She now needed a larger mirror. Long before Shirley Conran espoused the principle of the 'Superwoman' who could 'have it all', here was a woman who did have it all – a career, a marriage, a family, and a United Kingdom with all its realms and territories. But, unfortunately, she would find that something had to give.

What all this meant for the young prince-duke is that he saw even less of his mother. She was driven by a sense of duty that had been instilled into her by the fine example her father had set during the dark years of the Second World War. For her the job would always come first.

(Later on Cha ingeniously overcame the lack of face-to-face time he enjoyed with his mother by always having a selection of newly minted coins hidden about his person that he could get out and stare at whenever he was feeling down. He was particularly fond of the half crown, but found the threepenny bits a little disconcerting.)

Not that the queen didn't try to move with the times and usher in a new era of informality within the royal household. After all it was she who insisted that Cha was no longer required to bow on entering the presence of the sovereign. (Admittedly everyone else still had to bow. They still do; there's no point in rushing these things.)

However, although it was little understood at the time, by far the most significant assault on royal deference took place on the very day that Cha's mother was crowned queen. Television cameras were allowed into Westminster Abbey to broadcast the ceremony to the nation. On the face of it this accommodation of ancient ritual to the possibilities for mass communication that television presented was a way of getting the whole nation to witness the spectacle and pay their respects. And in many ways it was just that. But, back then, very few people had any inkling how hungry a beast television, and the new media age it presaged, would become.

Cha, however, was oblivious of much that went on. All he can clearly recall is the glorious music, the dodgy haircut he was given for his trip to the Abbey, and that afterwards on the balcony of Buckingham Palace, as the rain-sodden crowds cheered, his father turned to him and didn't whisper, 'One day, son, all this will be yours. And, to be perfectly frank, I don't think you're up to it.'

When it came to fatherhood Prince Philip wasn't exactly what you could call a new man. He was more of a man's man. Though long-suppressed rumour also has it that he was occasionally a ladies' man.

Unfortunately for him his son was, in many ways, a sensitive and timid soul. And while Philip loved his son, he didn't understand him. Or understand how to help him grow into the young man he thought he would need to be to cope with the demands the future would undoubtedly place upon him. In his father's presence Cha was passive and easily cowed. Sometimes, in the face of paternal criticism, he even withdrew into himself so much that he wasn't so much cowed as lambed.

Frustrated that his son was so clearly not the mini-me he would have obviously have preferred, Prince Philip tried to toughen him up and set him on the straight and narrow by rebuking his failings and making fun of him. Strangely, this did little for the small boy's confidence.

Just before Cha was five part of the royal nursery suite was converted into a classroom. The toys were removed and replaced by a Glaswegian governess. She taught him the rudiments of reading, and writing, and found him a pupil of fragile ego who was far from being the most riveting riveter on the Clyde. But he did like drawing horses and dogs. And he enjoyed singing. It is thought that it is during this time that he first learned and sang the words of both 'I Belong tae Glasgee' and 'The Red Flag'. All of which came as quite a considerable surprise to his parents in April 1954 when he joined them in Malta after a separation of five months while they had been touring ten Commonwealth countries. It was the first of many trips abroad that would leave long and lasting impressions on the nascent revolutionary.

In the Grand Harbour at Valletta he stood alongside his mother as she took the salute and watched as the entire British fleet of aircraft carriers, cruisers, destroyers, frigates and submarines steamed past and sailed off into the sunset.

Back in London, even by the age of seven, history fascinated him. Hardly surprising as a lot of it was about his family. Maybe this interest is why he was repeatedly drawn to a Van Dyck portrait of his ancestor Charles I that was displayed in the living room propped up on the sideboard alongside other family pictures. Although, like the artist's later work in the film *Mary Poppins*, certain details in the portrayal seem of dubious provenance, it was the decision to depict the subject of the picture as the *Three Heads of Charles I* that subconsciously may well have had the most lasting effect. But whether at the time the young Cha understood that the future that lay before him would involve trying to both navigate and reconcile the three aspects of his life – the public, the private and the inner – is unrecorded.

No doubt, however, the revolutionary life of Charles I was something the boy long pondered over. After all it was Charles I who said in one of his greatest speeches,

> I must tell you that liberty and freedom (of the people) consists in having of Government, those laws by which their life and their goods may be most their own ...

Unfortunately for Charles I this stirring cri de coeur on the rights of the people also included the far from egalitarian sentiment,

> ... a sovereign is not a subject ...

and the clearly misguided,

> ... therefore I tell you I am the martyr of the
> people,

and was made on a scaffold outside Mansion House where, a few minutes later, his head was cut off by order of Parliament.

Mind you, small boys love all that kind of thing. Even if it did involve someone in the family. But in the black and white world of childhood two messages came through to Cha loud and clear. First, when a revolution comes, it pays to be on the side of the people. Second, if you give them the chance, the government is not averse to chopping your head off.

Just before his eighth birthday Cha's home schooling came to an end. As his governess delivered him to his 'pre-preparatory' school in West London she looked down with affection on a boy she had come to realise was polite, serious, lacking in confidence, but older than his years. Unfortunately for him, physically speaking, his ears always appeared older than the rest of him. And the ribbing he subsequently endured was a constant unfair elbowing of oppression that pained him greatly.

But as every true revolutionary guerrilla fighter knows, to win the battle you must not only find ways of turning the enemy's strengths into a weakness, but you must take your own weaknesses and turn them into a strength. So if throughout all your small years your big ears have been your Achilles heel, you must find a way to transform them into your best foot that you put resolutely forward. And Cha did just that. He learned to listen. And not just to the voices that those around him thought he should hear.

Hill House, the pre-prep school in question, was an egalitarian institution of the highest order. It was founded by a character known as the Colonel and aimed to give 'half the places to English children and half to non-English children'. In this way it was a visionary precursor of so many of today's inner-city London schools. It also set out to enable pupils to 'learn to live with boys and girls of other nationalities, to respect that which is unknown and often very foreign to them, and thus open the door into a world which each day becomes smaller'.

But perhaps the most tangible expression of the school's egalitarian ethos was that when Cha's class went swimming in the pool at Buckingham Palace the Colonel hired two black cabs to ferry them back and forth as if they were just another ordinary bunch of London school kids. Not only did this give Cha the chance to encounter the working classes who would one day be his subjects, but it also taught him a valuable lesson on the importance of supporting small, independent, family businesses. And it was a lesson that struck a truly resonant chord with him, even at this early age, because wasn't he himself in line to inherit a small, independent, family business of his own?

The school's motto was taken from Plutarch – 'A boy's mind is not a vessel to be filled, but a fire to be kindled.'* Cha, apparently, needed extra kindling. For a long time it was a case of a lot of smoke but not much fire. It wasn't helped by the fact that he was not particularly physically robust.

Colds were commonplace and tonsillitis was a recurring problem which meant he was often away from school. Eventually, when he was eight, he had his tonsils removed and they were preserved in a glass jar. For several months afterwards he carried them around with him everywhere. It has never been recorded why or how he was eventually separated from them.

Maybe Cha became so attached to his tonsils, even after they were no longer attached to him, because he grew up in a world where the more conventional bonds of early childhood were somewhat distorted. His mother was engulfed in a high-profile career and was often away on business. His father was in the navy and far from a comforting figure when he was home. And the relationships he formed with his nannies were, inevitably, temporary. On top of all that, where exactly was he supposed to call home? Sometimes the family lived in Buckingham Palace in London. Sometimes they lived in Windsor Castle in Berkshire. Sometimes

---

* Plutarch also wrote: 'A Roman divorced from his wife, being highly blamed by his friends, who demanded, 'Was she not chaste? Was she not fair? Was she not fruitful?' Holding out his shoe he asked them whether it was not new and well made. 'Yet,' he added, 'none of you can tell where it pinches me.' But that was probably a bit long for a motto. And would have been a bit too scarily prescient.

they lived in Sandringham House in Norfolk. And sometimes they lived in Balmoral Castle in Scotland. Filling in forms was a nightmare.

Maybe it is in part as a reaction to this itinerant, disruptive start that he later on began develop an almost spiritual attachment to both land and landscape. And maybe it is why he grew into that most fascinatingly contradictory of figures, a revolutionary who is sceptical of change.

In 1957 he was sent to board at Cheam School in Berkshire. It was a prospect that filled him with dread. He would have to sleep at night on a steel bed in a cold dormitory. He would be woken at 7.15 by the clanging of the school bell. Then, washed and dressed and with prayers said at eight, he would have to be inspected by matron before he could file past the headmaster and sit down for breakfast. Later, in a collection of sparsely furnished and frankly dilapidated classrooms, he would be taught from a most conventional curriculum with much of the emphasis on learning by rote.

He didn't fit in. He found it hard to mix with the other children and for the first few nights he would cry himself to sleep. He was, after all, not yet nine years old. The school had been the choice of his father, who had been there himself when he was nine and it's not as if the place had done him any harm. (Many years later he explained his choice of it for his son by saying,

Children may be indulged at home, but school

24

is expected to be a spartan and disciplined experience in the process of developing into self-controlled, considerate and independent adults.)

As the summer term was ending in 1958 Cha and some other boys were called into the headmaster's study to watch the televised closing of the Commonwealth Games in Cardiff. Slightly embarrassed, as it was his mother who made the final speech at the ceremony it can only be imagined what he felt when she announced,

> The British Empire and Commonwealth Games in the capital have made this a memorable year for the principality. I have therefore decided to mark it further by an act which will, I hope, give as much pleasure to all Welshmen as it does to me. I intend to create my son Charles Prince of Wales today. When he is grown up I will present him to you at Caernarfon.

No doubt it was meant as an expression of love and encouragement. But for a child of the temperament that Cha had, it was probably just another burden for him to bear. His official title was now His Royal Highness Prince Charles Philip Arthur George Keith, Prince of Wales and Earl of Chester, Duke of Cornwall, Duke of Rothesay, Earl of Carrick, Lord of the Isles and Baron of Renfrew, Prince and Great Steward of Scotland.

Hardly surprising, then, that his name was never on the school football team sheet.

He left Cheam School in 1962. He loathed his time there. And though it has been acknowledged that his mother knew of his misery it was decided that it was in his own best interest that he should persevere to the bitter end.

When Cha was driven away from the school for the last time it was with no regrets. The prospect of a long summer spent amidst the Highland glories of Balmoral lay before him. And although after that loomed the seemingly distant horizon of a new school, it surely must be one much better suited to his character, temperament and needs than Cheam had been.

Meanwhile, in Argentina

★ ★ ★

CHE GUEVARA'S MOTHER was a woman of considerable pedigree called Celia de la Serna. Her paternal grandfather had been a wealthy landowner. Her father was a famous lawyer, congressman and ambassador. And she was in line to inherit revenue-producing estates when she turned twenty-one.

Che's father was a man called Ernesto Guevara Lynch. Although he was descended from an equally impressive line as his wife, by the time of his generation most of the family fortune had been lost.

When they met, Ernesto had invested what little money he had in a yacht-building company. But now, however, he was keen on another venture. The plan was to buy up a tract of jungle land and convert it into a yerba mate plantation. As yerba mate was used to make Argentina's national drink – the equivalent of tea in Britain – Ernesto was sure that the idea was bound to be a success.

At first the marriage proposal was opposed by Celia's family. The couple, however, were determined and eloped. Eventually Celia's family, seeing that in reality they had no choice, gave in and approved the union. Just as well as by now Celia was already pregnant.

After applying to court to get Celia's inheritance released early as she was not yet twenty-one, the newly married couple invested the money in 500 acres of jungle on the banks of the Rio Parana. They set up home in a place called Puerto Caraguati and appeared to at least one of the locals as 'rich and elegant people' who lived in a 'mansion'.

As the pregnancy progressed it was decided that the baby should be born close to better medical facilities and so Ernesto and Celia set off downriver. They got as far as the port city of Rosario. On 14 May 1928 the baby was born. He was christened Ernesto Guevara de la Serna. But he would come to be known to the world by an altogether shorter name. Che.

The family returned to the nascent plantation and Ernesto senior set to work to make the place a success. But it was a struggle. And although he reimbursed them in cash (for which he is fondly remembered), Ernesto Lynch still paid local Guarani Indian labourers a pittance for their long days spent clearing and planting the jungle.

In 1929, when Celia became pregnant again, a nanny was hired to look after the young Che. She stayed with the family for eight years. Shortly afterwards the family moved back to Buenos Aires so that Ernesto could sort out the boat-building investment which had got into financial difficulties. Little did they know that they would never return to the jungle. But Che did. In 1968. In Bolivia.

Soon after they settled down in Buenos Aires the boatyard was destroyed in a fire. Unfortunately for Ernesto Lynch his partner in the business had forgotten to pay the insurance premiums. So 1930 saw Ernesto's small inheritance go up in smoke. Not that he seemed particularly worried. That summer was spent cruising around islands on a forty-foot motor yacht that he had been given, or with the family on the beach of the San Isidro Yacht Club, or visiting wealthy relatives on their country estates.

One day in May, just at the start of Argentinian winter, Celia took her young son swimming at the Yacht Club. It was cold and windy. By bedtime Che had developed a coughing fit. The doctor who was summoned suspected asthmatic bronchitis. Medicine, however, did little to help and several days later the young Che was diagnosed with chronic asthma. It was a condition that was to affect him for the rest of his life.

Ernesto blamed his wife for taking the boy swimming, although the condition was probably inherited genetically from his mother and the cold air and water of that May day merely triggered symptoms that would have emerged anyway at some point.

Realising that a return to the damp climate of the jungle would be disastrous for their son, the family moved to Córdoba in the central highlands. Then they relocated to nearby Alta Gracia, its fine dry climate having made it a popular place of convalescence for people with breathing problems. It would be the place where they would spend the next eleven years. And the settled home for all of Che's most formative ones.

The Happiest Days of Your Life

☆ ☆ ☆

IF CHA'S FATHER wasn't the most supportive of parents for his sensitive soul of a son, a far more benevolent male role model soon began to feature more prominently in his life. This was his great-uncle Lord Louis Mountbatten of Burma.* One of the common bonds that cemented the burgeoning relationship between the young prince and the old lord was a shared love of the outdoor life. This especially blossomed in the days they spent together on Mountbatten's Hampshire estate, Broadlands. They liked nothing better than to be out in the elements together, communing with the natural beauties of the landscape and admiring the gloriously intricate web of life of the indigenous flora and fauna.

And what better way to show your true appreciation of an animal than by killing it?

By the time the boy was nine he had shot his first grouse. And landed his first salmon. A year later he took part in the annual coot shoot. And as an eleven-year-

---

* It is unlikely that anyone consulted the Burmese about this.

old in 1960 he wrote to his great-uncle of the 'great fun' he had had shooting thirty-three pheasants, a partridge, a moorhen and a hare over the course of two days. Naturally, fox hunting was another favourite.

He also liked playing hide and seek.

But whatever he did he seemed never to be too far away from a paternal rebuke from a father who clearly preferred his younger and more boisterous sister. Given his father's own history and childhood, it's hardly surprising that enlightened parenting skills were not amongst his primary assets. Cha's grandfather, Prince Andrew of Greece, had got the blame for a military cock-up that cost many lives in a war with Turkey back in the 1920s. Subsequently Andrew was charged with treason by a 'Revolutionary Committee' and was in line for a firing squad. Luckily George V intervened and negotiated his release, a condition of which was the fairy-tale sounding 'perpetual banishment' from his homeland.

The family subsequently set up shop in a small villa in Paris. Prince Andrew then moved out to a smaller flat and brooded the rest of his life away. Then Philip's mother became ill and moved to a sanatorium in Switzerland, emerging only to become a nun and found her own religious order. Philip, the youngest of five children, was raised by his sisters until he was sent to Cheam School at nine.

He ended up in the Royal Navy and met a nice English girl called Elizabeth. As she was in line to be queen, in order to marry her he had to give up his own Greek titles, and also his Greek Orthodox faith, and become a member of the Church of England. After the marriage, though he was given the title His Royal Highness the Duke of Edinburgh, he often found himself treated with disdain by the court. And even after his wife became the monarch the sleights continued. If there was one thing the intricately class-obsessed British establishment excelled at, it was in subtly keeping foreigners in their place. It would be difficult to imagine a society more skilled in looking down on somebody they appeared to be looking up to.

All of which made Cha that most contemporary of phenomena, a dual-heritage child. Unfortunately it seems he grew up in an environment where only one half of his heritage was particularly valued.

All children have a sense of injustice. All children have an inbuilt conception of right and wrong. Visit any playground, in any country, in any age and eavesdrop on any dispute and before very long the same words will be heard: 'It's not fair'. To be a rebel, to grow up to be a revolutionary, somewhere along the line this innate sense of right and wrong has to be burned into your very being. The resolve to do something about injustice might come later, but an understanding that the world, by its very nature, is unfair is the fertile soil in which the seed of revolt will eventually grow.

By rights Cha should have gone to Eton. That's where trainee kings tended to be educated. Harrow, of course, was another option. But, in the end,

Gordonstoun was chosen, the school his father had attended after Cheam. One of the other reasons Eton was shunned and Gordonstoun chosen was explained by a commentator of the time like this:

What is unique about Eton is not the way it teaches Latin or maths but the fact that virtually all its pupils come either from the upper class or upper middle class ... Thus the significance of the decision not to send Prince Charles there ... but to send him instead to Gordonstoun is ... that he will be the first monarch to be educated in an institution which is fundamentally classless.

So, like so many other schoolchildren of the sixties, the boy who would grow up to be Cha was to 'enjoy' an education that had, in part at least, been designed to fulfil some idealised social engineering concept. Having said that, the term 'classless' is obviously a relative one in this case as the fees at Gordonstoun were actually higher than those at Eton. In addition the working classes of Britain, as well as not having the spare disposable income to choose private education, had historically never understood that the best way to express their love for their children was to send them away for long months at a stretch during their most formative and most vulnerable years.

Gordonstoun was set up on the banks of the Moray Firth in 1934 by a German, Dr Kurt Hahn. Hahn was Jewish and an active opponent of the rise of Nazism, hence had been forced to flee his home in southern Germany in 1933.

Among the school's founding ideals was the aim to,

> Build up the imagination of the boy of decision and the will power of the dreamer, so that in future wise men will have the nerve to lead and men of action will have the vision to imagine the consequences of their decisions.

Hahn also drew on the educational principles found in Plato's* timeless contemplation of political and moral philosophy *The Republic*, which had it that

> There will be no end to the troubles of states, or ... of humanity itself, till philosophers become kings in this world, or till those we now call kings and rulers truly become philosophers, and political power and philosophy thus come into the same hands.

With these thoughts in mind Hahn endeavoured

---

* It might be noted that Cha's first school modelled itself on Plutarch, and his second school held Plato as a guiding light. By rights, then, the university he went to should have been one where Pluto was the main philosophical guide. However, as Pluto was Mickey Mouse's dog and never said anything more profound than, 'Woof-woof, arf-arf, Grrrrrrr!', this seems to lack educational merit. On second thoughts, maybe this isn't too bad a summary of what university life in the sixties was like.

to create a school that would be an egalitarian society without internal hierarchies where merit and character were key, where self-discipline and self-reliance were central, and where just because you were born into a position of financial privilege didn't mean you could not become a believer in the ideal of social equality.

Unfortunately, by the time Charles got there in 1962 the ideals and the realities had long since parted company. The still shy, sensitive and insecure thirteen-year-old found himself thrust into a world where, once the lights went out in the dorms and the housemasters were nowhere to be seen, brute force and tribalism reigned.

Fearsome gangs of boys roamed the night attacking smaller victims. Both money and food were regularly stolen. New boys were often initiated into the way of the world by having the flesh on their arms pinched by a pair of pliers which were then slowly twisted. At other times victims were trussed up in large wicker laundry baskets and left under the cold showers for hours at a stretch.

Cha's housemaster, himself a strict disciplinarian with a volatile temper, no doubt aware that some kind of 'boisterousness' went on when his back was turned, warned the other boys in the house that anyone caught bullying Cha would be expelled. At which point the words 'red rag' and 'bull' would be most appropriate. If Gordonstoun was *Lord of the Flies* territory, then there was undoubtedly a new Piggy in town.

Anyone who sought to befriend Cha was soon

cruelly ostracised for sucking up or being a toady. On the quarter-mile walk to and from the main building where food was served no one would walk with him, let alone talk to him. Every night was an ordeal as he was hit continually. And even during the day ways were found to victimise him. During rugby matches, being not particularly sporty, Cha was easily tackled. As a scrum formed around him the fists and boots would fly with the honour of having punched the future King of England being greatly prized.

Two years into his time at the school things still hadn't improved, as a letter he wrote clearly reveals.

> It's such hell here, especially at night. I don't
> get any sleep practically at all nowadays ... They
> throw slippers all night long or hit me with
> pillows or rush across the room and hit me as hard
> as they can ...

But for reasons only known to himself he never complained about his treatment at the school to the teachers.

As well as an acute sense of injustice all revolutionaries need to be able to identify with the underdog. That's because all revolutions are fought to help the oppressed. In his time at Gordonstoun oppressed is precisely what Cha was. But it is because he was oppressed, and relentlessly so, that he began to learn that other vital requisite of every revolutionary – resilience.

The Foothills of a Revolutionary

★ ★ ★

BACK IN THE 1930S Alta Gracia was a lovely hillside resort of a few thousand people. It was surrounded by farms and open, unspoiled countryside and breathed pure, fresh, mountain air. As soon as the family got there the young Che's asthma improved.

Life for the family was like one long holiday. Celia loved nothing better than taking the children for long rides on the backs of mules, or to while away the afternoons on swimming expeditions to the local swimming holes.

Although still prone to the occasional asthmatic attack, Che's new vigour meant that he could live life to the full. And he did. He developed into a real handful who would run riot with a local gang of children. But his caring side was revealed in his burgeoning relationship with his youngest sister, whom he would take on walks and entertain with stories he either remembered or invented.

Though the family was perennially short of money, as the income from the yerba mate plantation had plummeted, life was good. This was because the cost of living in Alta Gracia was relatively low. Also, thanks to her inheritance, Celia had some residual income of her own. It was this that carried the Guevaras through much of the 1930s.

But, having said that the family were on a continuous tight budget, it did not stop them living beyond their means. Generous dinner parties were often thrown. Both an automobile and a riding trap were run. And summers were even spent at Argentina's exclusive seaside resort of Mar del Plata. All of which was par for the course of the well-to-do social scene of Alta Gracia in which the Guevaras had become firmly ensconced. They fitted right in as they obviously were from the right class, lived in the right style and boasted the right surnames. They also had the inborn confidence that a privileged upbringing was wont to instil.

Che's illness meant that he didn't go to a regular school until he was nine. Until then he had been tutored at home. By his mother. During the sessions they spent together the bond between them that was already strong became unbreakable. And it became even more obvious that they were similar people in so many ways. Both mother and son enjoyed excitement and danger, each was opinionated and decisive and, in their own ways, both Celia and Che loved to rebel.

Despite the improvement in his health that the mountain air and dry climate had encouraged, Che's asthma never stopped being a worry for his parents. To remedy it Ernesto and Celia tried everything. But nothing worked. The only way forward was to try to contain the condition. Diet became a primary weapon. And the discipline Che learned about what he could and couldn't eat, especially during an attack, was to stay with him for the rest of his life. Sometimes, just to get through to where you want to be, you have to suffer. It was a most useful lesson for a young revolutionary.

Often the attacks were so severe that Che couldn't walk and was confined to bed for days at a time. As the solitary hours stretched before him reading became his way of escape. He devoured everything that he could get his hands on. As his mother had a lot of books and was particularly enamoured of poetry, there was a lot to read.

When the attacks subsided Che launched himself into physical activity with abandon. He played football, he rode horses, he swam, he dammed streams, he hiked the hills and he stood firm in the rock fights that were arranged between rival gangs. In short, whenever his body allowed him to he devoured life just as voraciously as he devoured books.

Apart from his illness the only cloud on his horizon was that his parents no longer got on. Disagreements often escalated into arguments and ended up in shouting matches. But as divorce was not legal in 1930s Argentina, or maybe just for the sake of the children, they stayed together and tried to ride out the storms.

When Che hit nine years old the education authorities cut short his days of freedom by insisting that he went to school. His headmistress, who was forever spanking him for one transgression or another, remembers him as 'a mischievous, bright boy, undistinguished in class, but who exhibited leadership qualities in the playground'.

He was also a prankster and a show-off. He drank ink from a bottle, ate chalk, hung off the side of a railway bridge and confronted a frightening ram in a mock bullfight. Or a real ramfight. And in the feral camaraderie of a gang he was even more boisterous. One time he shot firecrackers through a neighbour's open window into the middle of a formal dinner party. Another time, to get even with a boy from a rival gang, he snuck into his rival's house and, dropping his trousers, added a third colour to the ebony and ivory keys of a grand piano.

Back at home an atmosphere that visitors saw as decidedly bohemian prevailed. Though the family enjoyed the privileges that their class bestowed they weren't hidebound by the social conventions. The friends that the children brought home at teatime were just as likely to be the sons of the local golf caddies as the offspring of fellow members of Alta Gracia society.

Celia challenged just what a lady of certain standing was allowed to do in other ways too. She wore trousers, she drove a car and she smoked cigarettes. She also embarked on a campaign to get the local schools to supply a daily cup of milk to all their pupils to help combat the poor nutrition that was rife. When the school board dragged its heels she got things rolling by paying for the milk herself.

Though Argentina was a long way from Europe, the turmoil of the 1930s soon touched even Alta Gracia. The Spanish Civil War was closely followed by many in the town and as Franco's fascists got the upper hand Republican refugees from the struggle began to arrive. The Guevara family befriended many of them. Then with Hitler's invasion of Poland Che's father Ernesto joined a group that supported the Allies. Che himself joined the organisation's youth wing. But in truth he was still just a boy and loved nothing better than running riot with his friends or burying his head in classic adventure stories by the likes of Jules Verne or Alexandre Dumas.

In 1943, with Che approaching the age of fifteen, the family moved back to Córdoba when Ernesto found a partner with whom to set up a building firm. For a while their fortunes looked up. They lived in a country chalet near the university and opposite the exclusive tennis club where the children, now five in number, learned to play.

Che, rushing headlong into the maelstrom that is adolescence, found himself drawn towards a group of friends that was older than himself. One of their number was Alberto Granado, a biochemistry student and coach of the local rugby team. Before long Che, though still comparatively small for his age, had secured a place in the team, a reputation as a fearless tackler and the nickname 'el Furibundo' (the Raging

One). In striking contrast to his on-pitch antics before practice sessions he could often be found sitting with his back against a goalpost reading Baudelaire, Freud, Steinbeck or Verlaine.

Clearly he was growing into a young man who had a hunger both for the excitements of the physical life and the stimulations of the intellectual one.

The Cooler King

☆ ☆ ☆

FOR CHA, AT GORDONSTOUN, education had turned into an ordeal. Survival was the order of the day. Constantly finding himself in a kind of mental solitary confinement he knew that whatever he did he would never be allowed to fit in. Inevitably he soon began devising plans for his escape.

In his first bid for freedom he borrowed a motorbike from a butcher's delivery boy who had come to the school to drop off half a hundredweight of haggis that every morning would be stirred into the gloopy morning porridge. Revving up the bike he raced across the fields and jumped over the fence that surrounded the school. Unfortunately as the bike landed the front wheel skidded on a sporran bush and bike and rider crashed to the ground.

His next bid for freedom involved creating a dummy of himself by stuffing a selection of his clothes with straw, carving a head out of a giant turnip and leaving the substitute in his bed while he crept away. Unfortunately Cha's deception was soon found out by his tormentors as, when the lights went out and the first pillow-wielding assault began, the victim's head, instead of stoically accepting the violence as normal, rolled onto the floor. The initial cheers of the attackers soon turned to cries of outrage and the real Cha was quickly hunted down.

In desperation the next day Cha hit on the idea of hiding out inside the school's vaulting horse and tunnelling out from underneath it. He would then dispose of the material he had dug out by hiding it in special pockets he had sewn into the legs of his trousers and, when no one was looking, emptying them on to the schools' flowerbeds. In many ways it was a brilliant plan. In one crucial way it was rather stupid.

The school's vaulting horse was in the gymnasium. So when Cha started tunnelling the first material he was digging out was wooden floorboards. Surreptitiously scattering shards of splintered floorboard onto a flowerbed turned out to be not as surreptitious a course of action as he had hoped. In later years his habit of always standing with his left hand in his pocket fiddling with something is an unconscious throwback to his time at Gordonstoun when he was trying to tunnel out of his torment. It also explains why this involuntary action is often seen when he is in the glare of the media spotlight.

Given that all his attempts at physical escape were doomed to failure it is hardly surprising that as his adolescence continued he was increasingly drawn to other worlds within which he could experience at least some kind of freedom.

Books became one way out. And it was a way out that was completely within his own control. Open a book and within its covers you could be spirited away to any place on earth, any time in history and even to worlds of pure imagination. Close the book and the world within will wait, exactly as you left it, until you open it again.

Art became another land in which Cha could enjoy exile. He spent many long hours in Gordonstoun's art room. Pottery was a particular favourite and, given the chance, he would while away long afternoons making really quite professional, somewhat humorous pots on the potter's wheel while he hummed to himself the tune of 'Unchained Melody'.

Songs from the pop charts, however, were not the real music he was interested in. At Cheam he had bashed out 'Chopsticks' on the piano, but had not taken to the instrument. At Gordonstoun he learned the trumpet and sang in the choir. But it was the cello with which he had a real affinity. In some people's opinion he could have been a really good player. If only he had kept up the practice. And if, in a classic example of his low self-esteem, he hadn't judged his own playing quite as harshly as he did.

That he was attracted to music at all was a rebellion in itself as back at home harmonies rarely filled the air. Which is no surprise since Cha's mother was every-where she went, for her entire life, always bombarded by the same, frankly, quite awful, tune.

Cha, somewhat uncharacteristically given his

shyness and diffidence, turned out to be an accomplished actor. Perhaps this was because people uncomfortable with themselves in public find it easier to be someone else. Anyway, the first play he went up for was *Henry V*. Despite being tailor-made for the lead role he was cast as Exeter. However, this time round at least, he did not have to wait long to be king. The next school play was *Macbeth*, in which Cha played the Thane of Cawdor with great sensitivity and a revolutionary Glaswegian accent that he had memorised and perfected from his days of home schooling with his meat-pie munching governess.

It was around this time too that he started to take an interest in religion. Whilst the teachings and traditions of the Church of England were things that gave him solace and a certain degree of identity he would, in later life, find them restrictive constraints against which to rebel.

But this would be the quietest of all the fronts upon which he would lead an assault. The attack, when it came, would be subtle, personal and most profound. He would move from a view of religion that one day would cast him, absurdly, as the head of the Anglican Church, to the view that what was really important were the twin pillars of spirituality and faith. But this lay years in the future. For now the Church was another place to escape to, another place to try and find some meaning.

Given all this, Cha's love of, and growing attachment to the countryside can be seen in a completely different context. The countryside was a place of physical, intellectual and spiritual escape. A world in which you could become totally absorbed, and within which the worries and pressures of daily life could disappear. And in the countryside who you were, and what you were duty bound to become, counted for nothing. You were just a single soul and had to accept that you were of no more significance than a leaf on a tree, or a shaft of sunlight falling on a kingfisher's wing.

The final place Cha escaped to was a world in which no order ruled and absurd logic governed the outcome of the most ridiculous of predicaments. It was the world of *The Goon Show*. *The Goon Show* was a madcap radio programme that originally ran throughout the 1950s and that brought surrealism and anarchy to a mainstream British public that was still suffering the long, grey, drab hangover of the Second World War. Once a week, for half an hour, its listeners were immersed in a world of mental slapstick, imaginary cartoonery, dreadful puns and silly voices.

Cha, tuning in to repeats in the 1960s, listened and fell in love with a world in which anything could happen and usually did. Thanks to records of the show he soon had mastered impressions of many of the voices it featured. And in a line of succession that runs from the Goons through Monty Python and Ali G to Vicky Pollard today he was, just like so many adolescents over the years, given to spouting his party piece at every possible opportunity.

What Cha little realised during all the time he was

treading his myriad escape routes was that, while they would never set him free, they would help him deal with his confinement.

Back at home the prospect of the duties that lay ahead of Cha were never far below the surface. What those duties actually meant were harder to convey. The key problem was that the whole concept of a constitutional monarchy was patently absurd. And maybe it was the very absurdity that led Queen Elizabeth, one Wednesday when it was raining and she was at a bit of a loose end rattling around Buck House in her dressing gown and slippers, to come up with a brilliant idea. Sitting down on a regal G-Plan sofa she rang a small bell at her elbow.*

In an instant an Apprentice Deputy Under-Footman put down the corgi he was polishing inside the sideboard and made haste to HM's environs. The queen issued her request and within minutes the extravagantly attired Apprentice Deputy Under-Footman was furiously peddling his two-wheeled tricycle in the general direction of Mr Spike Milligan's Bakelite yurt.

Mr Spike Milligan was the comic genius who wrote most of the scripts of *The Goon Show*. The mad world that he, week in, week out, created was very much his way of escaping the allegedly sane world that he, week in, week out, found himself living in during the 1950s.

---

* A strange place for a bell, but perhaps royal physiology differs from yours and mine.

What follows is a reasonably accurate transcript of *The Goon Show* that was specially commissioned by the queen from Mr Spike Milligan to help explain to her son the point of the royal family. Its aim was to get the lad to understand where he stood. (And why while he stood, others would often kneel, or at the very least curtsey.)

The show – the now famous 'Dreaded Affair of the Pointless Crown', was never broadcast on air, or even in the air, but instead was performed in a one-off performance at the Palace for all the members of the royal family.

'The Dreaded Affair of the Pointless Crown'

A CHARACTER LIST IS given below and is followed by the script itself.

Characters

Neddy Seagoon	Main protagonist, cheerful, patriotic, gullible, easily swindled. Played by Harry Secombe.
Eccles	A ragged idiot based on Walt Disney's Goofy. Played by Mr Spike Milligan.
Bluebottle	A simple, enthusiastic Boy Scout. Tendency to read out stage directions. Makes weapons out of cardboard and string. Played by Peter Sellers.
Hercules Grytpype-Thynne	Public school villain and cad. Played by Peter Sellers.

Jim Moriarty Oftentimes sidekick to Grytpype-Thynne.
Played by Mr Spike Milligan.

Announcer The voice of reason. Sort of.
Played by BBC staff announcer Wallace
Greenslade.

Sound Almost a character in themselves.
Effects (SFX) Brilliantly imagined and deployed to make
the impossible hilariously believable.

Also in this particular By Royal Appointment *Goon Show* Peter Sellers played both the queen and a squeaky-voiced Prince Cha.

Before you read the script, to give you some idea of just how radically surreal *The Goon Show* was at the time, just imagine that you live in a dull depressing world, where nothing exciting happens, where every-thing you do is regimented by conventions and forces over which you have no control, and your job – if you have one – is nothing but a daily grind that does little more than enable you to plod ever more wearily one step nearer the grave.

Well, that didn't take too long, did it?

Announcer This is the BBC Home Service.

Secombe And why not?

Milligan Why not? Why not? I'll tell you why not.

Sellers Why not?

SFX	*Regal fanfare.*
Announcer	Mea culpa, mea culpa, this is the BBC *Palace* Service, mea maxima culpa.
Milligan	That's why not.
Announcer	Yes, by special request of Her Royal Ha-Ha-Ha-ness the Queen …
SFX	*Guillotine dropping, head being cut off and hitting the floor.*
Milligan	Later, later you fool.
Announcer	… The Bikini Atoll Light Operatic Society loudly present the esteemed, but as yet undecorated, Goon Show players in …
SFX	*Dramatic orchestra chords.*
Announcer	… 'The Dreaded Affair of the Pointless Crown'.
SFX	*Distant war whoops mixed with chickens clucking.*
Seagoon	It was 1959 and I had been summoned to the Palace. It was 1961 by the time I got there. That's the last time I go through Penge during rush hour. I rang the doorbell.
SFX	*Doorbell. Large door creaking open.*
Queen	Yeeessss?

Seagoon	I have come to see the queen.
Queen	Is there a flag flying on my head?
Seagoon	Yes.
Queen	Then I am in. Follow me.
SFX	*Heavy hobnail boots head off down long corridor.*
Queen	(*In distance*) Well, come on then.
SFX	*Pitter-patter of Seagoon's tiny footsteps following down the corridor.*
Seagoon	We came into a large, ornate room in which stood a large, ornate, army-surplus style throne. As the queen sat down …
SFX	Lone bagpipe plays opening bars of national anthem.
Queen	Not now, Mother.
Seagoon	From behind the army-surplus style throne an army-surplus style Queen Mother, cradling a bagpipe, shot out on an ermine covered pogo stick.
SFX	*Boing, boing, boing … (diminishes into distance) … Distant splash.*
Queen	Monsieur Seagoon, I summon you hear on a matter of national impotence.
Seagoon	I was all ears.

Milligan	Which was very eerie, folks!
Queen	It is One's Boy. Last night he entered One's bedchamber with One's crown on his head, pointed to it with his Dymo Label Maker and said, 'Mummy, it's pointless.'
Seagoon	At that very instant, from out of a small coffee bar in the corner of the room, an even smaller character stepped with a crown on his bonce. As he approached ...
SFX	*Footsteps on gravel.*
Seagoon	... I could see with my own eyes, but the National Health's glasses, that the crown was indeed ... without points!
SFX	*Orchestral horror chord.*
Seagoon	With that, the queen had me sign an inflatable kipper printed with the terms and conditions of my employment, then, boarding a number 37 bus bound for the Small Banqueting Hall, wished me good luck in my quest for the missing points of the crown.
SFX	*Bus bell rung twice. Bus drives away.*
Seagoon	Needle-nardle-noo. I had to get to the bottom of things. I headed for the bowels of the Palace.
SFX	*Footsteps going downstairs.*

Seagoon	Past the lungs of the Palace.
SFX	*Footsteps going downstairs.*
Seagoon	Past the kidneys.
SFX	*Footsteps going downstairs.*
Seagoon	Ignored the door marked 'spleen' as it sounded like a large convention was taking place in there. Aha, the door marked 'Bowels'.
SFX	*Door opening. A raspberry.*
Seagoon	Was that you?
Eccles	No, dis is me.
Seagoon	You're very small.
Eccles	I'm a footman.
Seagoon	But you have two feet.
Eccles	I'm working overtime.
Bluebottle	And I too am a footman. Steps out of shadows to reveal himself. Awaits applause. Not a sausinge. Stops revealing himself.
Seagoon	My good fellows, I come in search of the missing points of the crown.
Bluebottle	Steps forward. Whispers confidently. You have come to the right place. We have all the right answers. Steps back.

Eccles	Yersss.
Seagoon	That's good because I have all the wrong questions. Question one.
Bluebottle	I am glad you askeded that question. The queen is a symbol of the nation.
SFX	*Large cymbals crash together.*
Bluebottle	And because she is independent of party politics she can represent the whole nation, not just small clementine-style segments of it. Which is most useful at national ceremomonies and bar mitzvahs, etcetera.
Seagoon	A symbol, you say?
Eccles	Yup.
Seagoon	Not a triangle?
SFX	*Triangle being struck.*
Eccles	Nope.
Seagoon	Or a bassoon?
SFX	*Swanee whistle.*
Eccles	Nope.
Bluebottle	Slightly miffed and thinking of rude sailor word. No, my good man, she is a symbol.
SFX	*Cymbal.*

Seagoon	I see. Question two.
Bluebottle	I am glad you askeded that. The queen acts as a check on the governingment. Not a big check –
Eccles	Dat sounds like da BBC.
Bluebottle	– it is more like a pause for thought. Pauses for thought. Can't think of anything. Waits for next line.
Seagoon	How does the queen make the governingment pause for thought?
Bluebottle	Well, my valley-cradled friend, she does this because of her three rights she has on the doingses of the governingment. The right to be consulted. The right to advise. And the right to warm.
SFX	*Air raid siren.*
Seagoon	But does the prime minuscule have to follow her advice? Or heed her warmings?
Bluebottle	No. But he has to listen.
Seagoon	Is it fair that she has this power when no one has elected her?
Bluebottle	But she does not have power, she has influence. And, what is less, she only has influence so long as she doesn't really appear to influence anything. And

	anyway, as everyone knows, two rights (plus one) don't make a wrong.
Eccles	Yup. But three rights make a left.
Seagoon	I see. Question four.
Bluebottle	You rotten swine. That is a silly question. Gives stern look. Accepts sheepish expression …
SFX	*Baaa!*
Bluebottle	… in return. Instead I will answer question five, part two. First she takes the royal spittoon and fills it with water from the River Jordan.
SFX	*Water filling large vessel.*
Bluebottle	Then she takes the Houses of Parlingment and rolls it into a small ball.
SFX	*Houses of Parliament being rolled into a small ball.*
Bluebottle	Then she drops the ball into the spittoon and swirls it around with a handy Black Rod-style staff until it is completely dissolveded.
SFX	*Big splash. Water being swirled.*
Seagoon	With that Bluebottle leaned over the spittoon to check that Parlingment had indeed been dissolved when –

SFX	*Splash.*
Bluebottle	I don't like this game.
Eccles	He's fallen in the water.
Bluebottle	Help! Help! Splashes splashily in water to show distress. I don't want to be deaded by drowneding.
Seagoon	Thinking fast I threw him a Mae West. Thinking slow he threw me a Diana Dors. I was just about to settle the matter by seeing his Diana Dors and raising him a Sabrina when a small trapdoor opened in the floor and a small trap appeared. Caught in the trap were as dastardly a pair of ne'er-do-wells as I had ever seen this side of the Golders Green ferret crematorium.
Grytpype -Thynne	Hello. Grytpype-Thynne here. Comrade Hercules Grytpype-Thynne, left-wing intellectual and polytechnic lecherer in Tweed.
Seagoon	With him was the notorious 'Fleet Street' Jim Moriarty, press baroness and editor-in-crimpeline of the *Daily Chip Wrapper*.
Moriarty	Hold the front page. New headline. 'Never Dig Tunnels In Stilettos.'
Seagoon	What are you two doing under the Palace?

Grytpype-Thynne	My plan is a simple one.
Eccles	Dat's my most favourite type of plan.
Grytpype-Thynne	Using my cunning cunning I will destroy the legitimacy of the monarchy by sidling up to people in bus queues and tapping out on their knees the Morse code message ...
SFX	*Manic Morse code signalling.*
Grytpype-Thynne	... that royalty is an anachronistic waste of money holding the country back in a stifling world of deference and unearned privilege. Meanwhile ...
Moriarty	Meanwhile I will marshal the forces of the new media age to first praise all things royal then, when their guard is down, I will pull back the Antimacassar of Mystery that surrounds them and reveal them to be nothing more than an inbred, blue-blooded version of *Mrs Dale's Diary* fit for nothing more than to be used as tabloid fodder in a vicious circulation war.
Seagoon	But why the tunnel?
Grytpype-Thynne	Plan B. We dig a shaft under Buck House and they all fall into a big hole.

Seagoon	Grytpype, you fiend! And what will you do after you've secretly undermined the monarchy?
Grytpype -Thynne	I will change my name to Fred, declare myself president, sell the country to the second highest bidder and with the proceeds retire to a small caravan located in the west shrubbery of the South Balham Gas Board.
Seagoon	Why the second highest bidder?
Grytpype -Thynne	I'm not greedy.
Seagoon	But your secret plan will never work, you fool. Where will you hide the soil from the tunnel?
Grytpype -Thynne	Tell him, Moriarty.
Moriarty	We'll dig another tunnel and bury it there.
Seagoon	Aha! But what about the soil from the second tunnel?
Grytpype -Thynne	Tell him, Moriarty.
Moriarty	We will make the second tunnel twice as big.
Seagoon	Curses! They had thought of everything.

Grytpype -Thynne	Look I've even chosen the net curtains for the caravan.
SFX	*Net curtain.*
Seagoon	At last he had made a mistake! Seeing my chance I seized the net curtains and used them to fish Bluebottle out of the royal spittoon.
SFX	*Dramatic orchestra chord.*
Bluebottle	Not so fast, Grytpype-Thynne! Assumes threatening boxing-type stance, while drying himself off with small packet of custard creams.
Moriarty	What about me?
Bluebottle	Oh sorry. Not so fast Grytpype-Thynne and Moriarty!
Moriarty	Thank you.
Bluebottle	You're welcome.
Eccles	Dur, what about me?
Bluebottle	You're on our side, Eccles. Looks askance at sidekick.
Eccles	Oh yerr.
Seagoon	It was a stand-off. Us against them. Three against two. Accrington Stanley against Accrington Livingstone. I had discovered the missing points of the crown, only

to find that the very institution of the monarchy was about to be fiendishly destroyed by Grytpype-Thynne from the left and Moriarty from the right.

Grytpype -Thynne   Moriarty get the reusable dynamite.

Seagoon   Quick as a flasher Moriarty unbuttoned his trousers and whipped out a large stick of reusable dynamite (unused).

SFX   *Match being struck. Fuse burning down.*

Bluebottle   Not so fast! Same line as twice before. Slightly different delivery. Unscrews elbows, removes home-made cardboard Swiss army spoon and a bowl of rice pudding.

Seagoon   In a blur of inactivity, Bluebottle took aim with a spoonful of rice pudding and flicked it at the burning fuse …

SFX   *Massive explosion.*

Bluebottle   Missed!

SFX   *Collapsing building. Breaking glass.*

Seagoon   The explosion had blasted us all back into the Throne Room. The queen, a little dustier than before, sat on the throne, and from under it protruded the ruby-slippered feet of Grytpype-Thynne and Moriarty.

Queen   One will miss the old Palace, but it was probably time to renovate.

Seagoon   With that she pulled a book of wallpaper samples out of her handbag and was pondering a design with a corgi and macaroon motif when a small boy wearing a pointless crown appeared astride a blue toy elephant.

Bluebottle   Hello, Your Royal Not-Very-High-Yetness. Kneels down. Awaits knighthood. Still not a sausinge. Not even an obe.

Eccles   Hello, Little Prince.

Little Prince Hee-hee-hee. And now for the long reign whether forecast. By morning promiscuity will be widespread, but it will lift, and may give way to some hill snog. Virility will at first be poor … A manic depression over Ireland … A warm front followed by a cold back. Hee-hee-hee.

Queen   One does worry about him sometimes.

Seagoon   And then in a blinding royal flush of perspiration, The Dreaded Affair of the Pointless Crown was solved.

Eccles   Derr, tell me, Little Prince, why is your crown upside down?

Little Prince It is because if I wear it the other way up my dear Papa uses me as a coat stand.

Milligan	Sounds reasonable to me, folks!
Seagoon	What, what, what? So there had been points to the crown all along. You just have to make sure you wear the thing the right way up!
SFX	*National anthem being played on 73 kazoos. Fades down.*
Announcer	That was *The Goon Show*. And you, my allegedly royal listeners, have been, and will be, The Go On Show, because frankly what else is there for you to do?
Seagoon	You must go on.
Queen	I can't go on.
Seagoon	Shall I sing?
Queen	I'll go on.
SFX	*National anthem fades up. Plays till finish.*
Milligan	Taxi!

When it was explained to him like this Cha soon got the full measure of the magnitude of the madness that he would become increasingly involved in.

An Argentinian Adolescence

★ ★ ★

SHORTLY AFTER THE GUEVARAS moved to Córdoba in 1943 a military coup overthrew the president of the country. The new regime, led by General Pedro Ramirez, tried to suppress all dissent, including student protest. Alberto Granado, Che's friend, was locked up. When he asked Che to join a march demanding his release Che replied that he would do so only if he had a revolver. He expressly didn't want to be just another student on a march who would 'get the shit beaten out of them with truncheons'.

The talk of the revolver was probably bravado. In truth the fifteen-year-old was not yet motivated by politics. He briefly involved himself with Nazi 'hunting', but this was just yet another boyish adventure rather than a considered commitment to a political cause. As Che himself has written, 'I had no social preoccupations in my adolescence and had no participation in the political or student struggles in Argentina.'

This was an Argentina in which increasingly Juan Perón was moving to the fore and, before long, would become the president.

If politics held little real interest for Che the same could not be said for the pleasures that the opposite sex tantalisingly offered. In terms of sexual mores the country was still conservative and Catholic society still set the social rules. While the 'good girls' of his own social class were out of bounds, those from lower classes were not. For many young men of Che's background the first experience of sex was with the family's *mucama*, or servant girl. These were usually Indians from the interior or poor mestizas from one of Argentina's northern provinces.

For Che the opportunity arose one day when he was visiting a friend's house where a pliant maid worked. His efforts were monitored by a group of friends through the keyhole of the bedroom. And though his performance was most enthusiastic, it was his periodic pauses to suck on his asthma inhaler that left the most lasting impression.

A few years later it could be seen that a more romantic approach to love had flowered in him when a pretty younger cousin turned up for the summer holidays. Her father was a poet and he would try to woo her by reciting verses from Pablo Neruda's *Twenty Poems of Love and a Desperate Song*. She soon fell for him, but she was only one among many as he had grown into a good-looking young man with intense brown eyes and an easy self-confidence.

On top of all this he cast himself as an irrepressible rascal and an outsider. He was intelligent, he was funny, he derided social order and formality and, in a world where young men loved to wear good clothes, he cared little for how he dressed. And he gathered for himself more than one nickname. Sometimes he was 'el Loco' – meaning 'Crazy'. And sometimes, because of his reluctance to wash, he was 'el Chancho' – 'the Pig'. But in many ways the nickname that would have suited him best wouldn't be heard for another ten years. He was, quite definitely, a 'rebel without a cause'.

Another Prawn on the Barbie

☆ ☆ ☆

WHEN CHA WAS SEVENTEEN it was decided that he should take time out from Gordonstoun and spend a term at Timbertop, an associate school in Australia 100 miles north-east of Melbourne. It was established on the same principles as the school in Scotland, but had more of an accent on the outdoors and on learning self-reliance. At Timbertop there would be days at a stretch when the pupils had to fend for themselves, prepare their own food, cut forest trees for heating and sleep out in the freezing night air.

Given his ordeal at Gordonstoun he approached the prospect with a fair amount of trepidation. But he was soon to discover that his own 'transportation' was not as daunting a sentence as he at first feared.

In a country that supposedly had less class and culture than his own he found that fellow pupils were more willing to relate to him on account of who he was, not what he was. He discovered the pleasures of being just a schoolboy. And he discovered that school was somewhere that could be enjoyed.

On one trek, with temperatures often hitting ninety

degrees, he walked seventy miles in three days. At other times he bunked off revising for exams to fish for trout in a nearby stream. And to amuse himself, and others, he unleashed his *Goon Show* impressions.

He enjoyed the school so much that he informed his parents that he did want to stay on for a second term, as had been mooted as a possibility when he had first gone out. One of the main reasons for staying was the prospect of a school trip to Papua New Guinea.

If Gordonstoun had been in large part an encounter with a tribal society that had gone bad, Dogura in Papua New Guinea was a meeting with a tribal society that still held true to many of its old values and beliefs. The boy who was accumulating the information that would one day help transform him into a revolutionary spent four days at Dogura feasting, dancing, throwing spears and not just observing, but participating in a world so different from his own. He also worshipped at the local Anglican cathedral, listened intently to cases of faith healing and expressed concern that maybe the younger Papuans by rushing to embrace all things Western were losing an important part of their identity.

When he returned to Britain at the end of his two-term sabbatical he had changed. He had learned self-reliance and he had grown in confidence. He still faced the prospect of returning to Gordonstoun with some nervousness, but now he seemed more able not only to cope, but maybe even to prosper. And he did. He became the head of his house (much to his mother's surprise) and even head boy of the school. No doubt the fact that he would one day be king influenced the headmaster in some way, but in other ways it was a justifiable choice. And in a sentiment that could be taken to describe much of his life to come he wrote to his great-uncle Mountbatten about his new position:

> I don't know that I am doing my job very well as
> it is a rather vaguely defined one ... but I hope I
> shall get the hang of it as term goes on ...

By all accounts he acquitted himself well as head boy. He even brought a much needed degree of sympathy and compassion in his role as an intermediary between the staff and the pupils. But despite his inclusion into the ruling hierarchy of the school he never warmed to the place. Given his early experiences there this is hardly surprising. He left the school after six years with no regrets.

He also had two respectable A-level passes and gained an excellent result in a special paper in history. Years later he would come to realise that looking backwards was one of the best ways of looking forward.

The Reader

★ ★ ★

IN 1945, as the Second World War was drawing to a close, the seventeen-year-old Che began to show the depth that his enquiring mind was developing. He took a course in philosophy. He got 'outstanding' grades. So interested was he in the subject that he began to compile his own 'philosophical dictionary'. He wrote it by hand and in the end it ran to 165 pages. Its scope was impressive, covering everything from love to death, from neurosis to mortality, from reason to God. It included brief biographies of great thinkers and culled illustrative quotes from a vast array of source material.

There were extracts from Sigmund Freud's *General Theory of Memory*, Bertrand Russell's *Old and New Sexual Morality*, H. G. Wells's *Brief History of the World* and Adolf Hitler's *Mein Kampf*. Other quotes revealed that he had read Nehru, Nietzsche and Marx, Engels and Lenin.

What is equally striking in the vast range of his reading list is that he could see that both fiction and poetry gave valuable insights into how the world worked, and why, in many ways, and in many places, it didn't. In between grappling with the ideas of the great thinkers he read the novels of the great writers. Faulkner, Kafka, Camus and Sartre all featured heavily. And poetry too gave him another window on the world as he read translations of Walt Whitman and Robert Frost, but was particularly drawn to the Spanish Republican poets García Lorca, Alberti and Mercado.

To counterbalance the fact that so much of what he read was set in or grew out of either the old world of Europe, or the new world of North America, Che made it a point of seeking out Latin American authors. And in their novels and poems he gained insight into the inequalities of the lives of the people who lived around him but who were marginalised from the relatively gilded lives of his own social group.

Once again his mother proved a key influence in helping him see that there was more to the world than just the people and lifestyles of the class that they had been born into. She opened the doors of her home wide and welcomed in a panoply of people paying little heed to what was socially acceptable at the time. And whoever her children brought back with them at the end of the day would join the family to eat, with whatever was on offer just being divided up into smaller portions so that everybody got a share.

Given the glorious cultural mêlée at home Che often found that both space and peace in which to sit down and read were often in decidedly short supply. He solved the problem by hiring a small back room in a nearby hotel, next to the bus station, where he could study undisturbed. Obviously, being of an age when both hormones and testosterone were charging round his body, studying might not have been all he got up to in that bolt-hole.

While Che's mind roamed freely across a vast pampas of ideas, the need to focus his academic studies towards a career that would provide a living became a priority. This was especially true as by 1947 the family had moved back to Buenos Aires, his parents had decided to split up and, following a succession of commercial setbacks, money was so tight that Che's father had been unable to pay his taxes. The family even found themselves having to stay in his paternal grandmother's fifth-floor apartment.

No doubt with all this in mind, and since he was good at maths and science, Che had decided to study engineering when he went to university. After leaving school he even did a course in soil science and found work inspecting materials on a road-building project 150 kilometres north of the capital.

But in May of that year Che received a telegram saying that his 96-year-old grandmother had fallen ill. She had had a stroke and wouldn't survive much longer. Che quit his job and rushed to her bedside. He stayed with her for the seventeen days that it took her to die. And when she did die he was inconsolable with grief.

In the aftermath of the death of his beloved grandmother Che told his parents that when he went to university, instead of studying engineering, he was going to study medicine.

University Challenged

☆ ☆ ☆

WHEN CHA LEFT SCHOOL in 1967 he emerged into a world on the cusp of the state of an ever changing and fast evolving flux of often quite quantum leapian dimensions that represented paridigmical shifts that would define, redefine, then redefine the redefinitions at bewildering speed. England had lost an empire, but won a World Cup.* And the old social order seemed on the verge of dissolving in a cloud of marijuana smoke and to the sound of 'Lucy in the Sky with Diamonds'.

Blah blah blah. Blah blah blah . Blah blah blah blah blah Bob Dylan. Blah blah blah blah blah the pill. Blah blah blah Vietnam. Blah blah blah The Paris Riots blah blah blah The Grovesnor Square Pushing and Shoving. Blah blah blah Cold War blah blah Prague Spring. Blah blah blah Woodstock blah blah flowers in their hair blah blah but blah blah Altamont? Blah blah blah satire boom. Blah *That Was the Week that*

---

* It is interesting to note that these days nostalgia for lost empire and the Golden Age it represented has been replaced by nostalgia for the 1966 World Cup and the Golden Age it represented.

Was. Blah blah blah David Bailey blah blah mini skirts and Afros. Blah blah blah Hendrix, blah blah blah Janis Joplin, blah blah blah Martin Luther King. Blah blah blah grassy knoll blah blah blah book depository in Dallas. Blah blah blah 'One small step for man, one giant leap for mankind' blah! But blah blah blah in Britain blah blah Wonderloaf and Engelbert Humperdinck. Blah blah blah blah blah blah Alan Bennett in *Forty Years On*:

> To Let. A valuable site at the crossroads of the
> world. At present on offer to European clients.
> Outlying portions of the estate already disposed
> of to sitting tenants. Of some historic and period
> interest. Some alterations and improvements
> necessary.

Blah blah blah blah blah. Blah blah. Blah. With a Mars Bar. And a packet of crisps with a bag of salt in it!

It was in this contradictory world that the contradictory Cha would have to go to university. In the interest of keeping the monarchy abreast of the modern world his father decided that he should attend the hotbed of student turmoil that was the London School of Economics. Unfortunately at his interview the tutor in charge spotted that under his afghan coat and grubby kaftan he was wearing a pair of brogues. Things went further downhill when Cha pointed out that the joint another one of the tutors had rolled was being passed the wrong way round the table.

He went to Cambridge instead.

As to what subject he should study that proved to be another hot potato. In the end it was decided that what would be best for him would be a course tailored to suit his needs as heir to the throne. What is reproduced below, for the first time, is a confidential outline of the main modules of the proposed BA course in Pure and Applied Kingology.

1. Hand shaking.
2. Small talk.
3. Looking busy.
4. Waving.
5. Not waving (poetry module).
6. Practical sword dubbing & medal pinning.
7. Colour trooping.
8. Tax avoidance.
9. Small talk with foreigners.
10. Not looking bored during interminable receptions.
11. Royal Variety Performance anti-buttock-cramp exercises.
12. Looking sad on solemn occasions.
13. What to say at Christmas.
14. Photo opportunities – approved poses.
15. Spouse selection.
16. Heir fathering.
17. Spare fathering.
18. Waiting.
19. Advanced waiting.
20. Salsa!

Useful though such a course would no doubt be, what those who advised the royal family had failed to realise was that Cha, though often still socially awkward and diffident, was beginning to know his own mind. And be willing to express it. In a show of rebellion that was to foreshadow so much of his character he told the Dean of his college that he could ' stuff your pointless course up your arse'.*

Instead he chose to study archaeology and anthropology. Which is the study of ancient ruins and primitive tribal societies. Obviously this had very little relevance to the monarchy, but it was a good indication of the topics that interested him.†

Despite this show of defiance and independence the powers that were being at the time were determined not to let this student prince completely sing his own song. Unknown to Cha his tutor drew up a list of student clubs and organisations that he was banned from joining. These included the Buddhist Society, the Fabian Society, the Heretics, the Marxist Society, Amnesty International and the Society for Anglo-Chinese Understanding.

As all revolutionaries know oppression is a foot that wears a heavy boot. But maybe the worst kind of oppression is the boot that the oppressed doesn't even know is resting on his neck. Though Cha was

---

* These may not have been his exact words.

† On second thoughts maybe ancient ruins and primitive tribal societies are exactly what the monarchy is about.

undoubtedly travelling towards a future as a rebel, he still had a long way to go.

For a brief period he found a travelling companion in a fellow student up from the valleys of Wales on a scholarship. Over mugs of coffee the socialist and the prince discussed the world and its ways late into the night. Whether the discussions planted a seed that would long lie dormant, or merely manured a cutting that was already in bud, or even ripped up an ancient hedgerow that stood in the way of large-scale industrial agriculture (as it were), only time would tell.

A lot of the rest of the time Cha would spend in the company of his peers. Hardly surprising as one day many of them would, in all likelihood, end up being made peers. Hunting, fishing and shooting featured frequently at weekends and proved common ground for a kind of hale and hearty camaraderie. But, in truth, it was a camaraderie that did not extend much below the surface. And it was below Cha's surface that he was starting to find himself.

Like many other students Cha got a part-time job while at university. Unfortunately by the time he thought to do this most of the public houses had a full complement of barmen. Luckily his mum pulled a few strings for him and in the long university holidays he made himself useful being a counsellor of state. This meant that when his mother was abroad he could fill in for her. In this capacity he travelled to Australia for the funeral of a prime minister, and was also roped in to making an official trip to Malta. It was hard, unglamorous, badly paid work, but someone had to do it.

Maybe it was because his time was spent either in serious study, or holding the fort for the family firm, or killing animals, or on his new love of polo, that much of the turmoil of the 1960s seemed to pass him by. This despite the fact that Cambridge did have its very own student riots. Unfortunately, while the rest of the world was rioting about Vietnam, or civil rights, or whatever it was precisely that the French were rioting about, Cambridge somewhat missed the boat by rioting over an issue that not many other people seemed especially bothered about. In the even somewhat quaintly named 'Garden House riot' a promotion for Greek tourism at a local hotel erupted into a violent protest against the military regime of the colonels in Greece.

Cha, though obviously nowhere near the hotel when the riot occurred, would have undoubtedly heard all about it. And he would have seen that despite the really quite immoderate language of some of the placards at the demonstration the colonels in Greece did not step down. It was to be a most useful lesson in the realities of rebellion that would serve him well later in his life.

Whether the fact that he was part Greek himself made him identify with the struggle in any form is unrecorded. And subsequent underground reports that have lately come to light suggesting that he had indeed instigated the protests are completely unsubstantiated. Having said that, the rallying cry of the Garden House rioters of 'Tally Ho!' has never really been adequately explained.

But one area in which Cha did experience the flavour of the times was on the stage. He joined the Dryden Society, his college's drama group. He acted in revues, including one in which he had a comic monologue as a weather forecaster that he had written himself. His other notable role was as the padre in Joe Orton's *Erpingham Camp*.

The play, which had originally been commissioned by Rediffusion Television, was set in a south-coast holiday camp and shows how a small misunderstanding brings about riot, rebellion and anarchy. It was also an allegory of contemporary Britain. The camp owner, Erpingham, represented the establishment, the padre represented the Church, and the camp guests represented the different social classes. A newspaper review of the television production described it as 'a perfectly annoying little play and quite untypical of the way English people behave on holiday'.

At the start of the play Erpingham is the pompous, dictatorial and small-minded ruler of the camp that he sees as his own private fiefdom. Orton had originally written the part with Arthur Lowe in mind. (And this was before he had played Captain Mainwaring.) Though Erpingham was a petty man he had grandiloquent plans for

Rows of Entertainment Centres down lovely, unspoiled bits of the coast, across deserted moorland and barren mountainside. The Earthly Paradise.

In addition, so enamoured is he with ersatz decorum that before changing his trousers in his office he asks the padre to cover up the portrait of the queen that hangs behind his desk.

The dramatic action of the play kicks off when a stand-in entertainments officer instigates a screaming competition between two of the female guests, then slaps one whom he considers is getting hysterical. This results in the woman's husband, the working-class Kenny, leading an insurrection against the authorities that run the camp.

Erpingham sees this as an unjustified attack on all the values he holds dear. Or as he puts it:

We've our traditions. And they're not to be
lightly cast aside at the whims of a handful of
troublemakers. I'll never agree to their demands.

He then orders the campers to be locked out of their chalets and denied food at the restaurant, adding:

This whole episode has been fermented by a
handful of intellectuals ... It is my intention to
defy the forces of anarchy with all that is best
in twentieth-century civilisation. I shall put a
record of Russ Conway onto the gram and browse
through a James Bond.

The guests reply by deciding to

… break open the stores. Take the means of supply into our own hands.

The padre is cast in the role of peacemaker between the two sides. But Kenny has been pushed too far.

I'm an ordinary man – I've no wish to be a leader – my only ambition is to rest in peace by my own fireside. But, in the life of every one of us, there comes a time when he must choose – whether to be treated in the manner of the bad old days. Or whether to take by force those common human rights which should be denied no man. A place to eat, food for our kids, and respect. That's all we ask. Is it too much?

The stores are stormed and the padre beaten up as the rebels march on to confront Erpingham. The padre kneels in prayer.

Oh, Merciful Father, in Thee we trust when dangers threaten. *(He is hit by an egg.)* As the little foxes gnaw at the roots of the vine, so anarchy weakens the fibres of society.

In the mêlée the floor of Erpingham's office collapses and he is killed. The play ends with his funeral and the staff and the rebels and the padre trying to come to terms with all that has happened and the new world they now find themselves in.

Cha may well have ended up with egg on his face, but no doubt the ideas and themes of the play and its exploration of the mechanics of rebellion also left him with plenty on his mind.

If Joe Orton's play was his closest brush with the political turmoil of the time, albeit a brush that was distanced by the very long handle of art, it didn't take long for him to be heading straight towards the centre of his very own storm.

The first of July 1969 was the date that had been set for his investiture as Prince of Wales. Many of the people in the principality were looking forward to the day as one of loyal celebration. But many people weren't. Where some saw the event as a symbol of national unity, others saw it as a symbol of national oppression. Obviously it didn't really help that as Cha himself admitted he'd 'hardly been to Wales'. (Even so, he could do a mean Harry Secombe impression.)

Given that included in the political turmoil of late-sixties Britain was a growing nationalist clamour, the very staging of the investiture was bound to be provocative. And the whole affair had party political dimensions too. The Conservative Party was against the push for greater national autonomy for Wales and Scotland as it feared this would lead to a break-up of the United Kingdom. The Labour Party was also against it as it relied heavily on returning Welsh and Scottish MPs during elections to give it any chance of winning a majority in the Westminster Parliament. Therefore what both parties hoped the investiture would do was to cement the relationship between the principality and the whole concept of a greater, united, nation.

All of which, in many ways, made Cha little more than a political pawn. And, arguably, it meant that his forthcoming investiture had more real significance than even the coronation of his own mother.

While the majority of the Welsh were against nationalism, or not for it enough to actually do much about it, there were worrying signs for the government that maybe the pressure for change was building. A Welsh Nationalist had won the Carmarthen by-election. And, more seriously, an RAF officer was badly injured by one of a series of bombs in Wales that could very easily have killed many people. Not long after this Cha himself was anonymously identified as a target of the nationalist extremists.

To smooth things over it was decided to send Cha to Aberystwyth university for a term.

It proved to be a very lonely time. It's hard to join a new world of students who have already had four terms to form into groups of friends. Even more so if everyone knows that you are only going to be there for one term. On top of that, Aberystwyth wasn't the kind of place that attracted students with an aristocratic background, so Cha had very little in common with those around him. And the fact that those immediately around him included plain clothes security men didn't do much to help either.

With the prospect of the investiture looming it was decided that it would be wise if Cha was to learn about the history of the country. Also he needed to be able to speak a little of the Welsh language, the adoption of which as an official language in Wales had become a key battleground for the nationalists.

To this end he was instructed by a tutor at the university who was a member of the Welsh Nationalist Party. By all accounts he studied hard. And he started to gain a different insight into why nationalism, why identifying yourself with where you come from, why the aspirations of ordinary people to belong, and why history and heritage and culture, can all be so important. If he had grown up with only the distorted view of these things that his privileged position provided, here was the same vista as seen from far nearer the foot of Snowdon.

A test of his scholarship came when, at the end of term, he had agreed to address the 6,000 people attending the Eisteddfod – the annual Welsh festival of poetry, drama and music. It would be his first ever public speech of any significance. And he agreed to deliver it in Welsh.

It was to become the setting for a historic uprising.

He worked hard on the speech and practised the intricacies of pronunciation endlessly. When he rose to speak he was filled with excitement tinged with a little dread of the consequences of making a 'linguistic blunder'. But before he could utter a single word a phalanx of nationalist demonstrators rose from their seats and started shouting and heckling.

Unsure what to do, Cha just stood his ground. Before long the sympathy of the rest of the crowd swung towards him.

From out of the masses elderly Welsh women arose wielding handbags and bore down on the protesters and drove them from the marquee like St Patrick driving out the snakes.* Mayhem reigned until the police moved in and helped to eject, or maybe to rescue, the nationalists. But even outside the protest continued as the demonstrators clambered onto the marquee and continued shouting and banging to disrupt the proceedings. As a result, when Cha finally approached the microphone he was applauded and cheered. The speech was a resounding success.

What's more important is that Cha had learned a subliminal lesson that was to serve him well in his later years as a rebel. A revolution will never succeed if all you have is an intellectual elite behind you. You must speak to the people, you must be at one with them, you must argue your case and bring them with you. Fail to do that, and your endeavour, no matter how righteous its cause, will be doomed.

In keeping with the growing mediafication of royalty the investiture was planned to be a 'television event'. What soon became apparent to those arranging the ceremony was that there wasn't a great deal of investiture-staging precedent upon which to draw. The show

---

* Yes, I know St Patrick did this in Ireland. For God's sake stop being so pedantic, it's only an analogy.

would have to be, largely, made to fit the occasion. Cha's Uncle Tony, the Earl of Snowdon, was handed the role as its main producer. About the only thing that was clear about the whole event was that too overt a military presence would be unwise and ran the risk of having the Welsh nationalists characterise the investiture as a celebration of colonial dominance.

In response Snowdon designed a simple pageant that was decidedly modern in feel and not overloaded with English historical references. It was also choreographed to appeal to the general public and aimed to 'speak their language'.

As Cha sat on a modernist throne made of Welsh slate and lava bread, protected from rain by a knitted wool canopy, the show kicked off. First up, in a segment inspired by Dr Jacob Brownoski's popular BBC2 television programme *It's a Knockout*, came a simplified version of the revolt of Owain Glyndwr. It was re-enacted on plastic sheeting covered in foam, with the Welsh rebels dressed in leek costumes and the English soldiers dressed as sides of beef.

Next a rugby ball was drop-kicked into the grounds of the castle by Barry John and caught by Harry Secombe, who split it open with a ceremonial miner's pick to reveal the coronet. Then, as the queen approached Cha to crown him with the coronet, a 200-strong Welsh male voice choir led by Shirley Bassey, sang a moving version of 'The Ying Tong Song' set to the tune of 'Bread Of Heaven'.

Finally, as the newly crowned Prince of Wales went

walkabout among his new people, a more populist note was struck as Tom Jones bounded on stage and belted out a specially rewritten version of his hit 'It's Not Unusual' that captured the excitement and significance of the day yet still managed to express some of the mixed feelings surrounding the event. It was a bravura performance that soon had the crowd whipped up into a royal frenzy and singing along:

It's not unusual to be ruled by anyone,
It's not unusual to be fooled by anyone,
But when we see you walking around with
   everyone,
It's not unusual to see us bow,
We wanna kow-tow …

The song ended with Cha returning to the podium as hundreds of Union Jack knickers were thrown onto the stage, each with a message of encouragement, welcome, and loyalty, embroidered onto it by members of the Welsh WI.

The whole event proved to be a great success. And not even the occasional muffled 'crump' of incendiary devices exploding in the distance could detract from, and indeed may have added to, the genuine warmth with which Charles was received as he toured the principality in the days that followed.

La Facultad de Medicina

★ ★ ★

THOUGH HIS FAMILY SUSPECTED it was his frustration at having to watch his grandmother die that led him to switch to medicine, Che himself never justified his decision in that way. Many years later, however, he did say that what he sought was a 'personal triumph' and that he 'dreamed of becoming a famous investigator … of working indefatigably to find something that could be definitely placed at the disposition of humanity'.

This attraction towards, and longing for, a destiny was a theme that was more explicitly revealed in a self-conscious, melodramatic, but nonetheless remarkably prescient poem that he had written a few months earlier which included the following lines:

> The bullets, what can the bullets do to me if
> My destiny is to die by drowning? But I am
> Going to overcome destiny. Destiny can be
> Achieved by willpower.
>
> Die, yes, but riddled with

Bullets, destroyed by the bayonets if not, no.
 Drowned, no.
A memory more lasting than my name
Is to fight, to die fighting.

Still, all eighteen-year-olds embarking on a university career idealistically dream of changing the world, don't they?

Soon after starting to study medicine Che became especially interested in allergy research. No doubt his own crippling asthma gave the subject particular fascination for him. Initially starting as a patient in a specialist allergy treatment clinic, it wasn't long before he was employed as an unpaid research assistant. The doctor in charge was so impressed with him that he nurtured high hopes that the youngster would one day make a name for himself in the field.

Ironically it was Che's very often debilitating condition that now played a crucial role in furthering his development. This is because when he was called up by Argentina's military draft, a move that would have taken him away from his studies for a year, his asthma was judged so severe that he was rejected as being of 'diminished physical abilities'. The decision that he was unfit for military service would prove even more ironic given how hard he was to drive himself, and how much physical discomfort and disability he would overcome, in the years that lay ahead of him as a rebel and one of the greatest soldiers of the twentieth century.

As well as pursuing his official academic studies, and helping with allergy research experiments at the clinic, Che also continued the philosophical readings that he had started as a teenager. Books on sexuality and social behaviour attracted him, as did those on social philosophy. But perhaps most significant was a focus that was developing on the concepts and origins of socialist thought. Stalin and Lenin and the Argentinian socialist Alfredo Palacios were all studied. But it was the writings of Karl Marx that really began to hold his attention.

Having said all this, it seems that his growing exploration of, and identification with, socialism was mainly one of intellectual curiosity. In his days at university he showed no interest in becoming in any way affiliated with the left, or involved in student politics. Indeed, friends at the time saw him as an ethical, not a political person.

As Che advanced with his studies Perón strengthened his grip on Argentina with a brand of populist politics that aspired to an 'organised community' of man living in harmony. Perón's wife Eva assumed an almost spiritual role that cast her as the dazzling 'soul' of the nation. Perón tried to create an international alignment for his country that he described as the 'Third Position'. It was to lie somewhere between the West and the East, between capitalism and communism.

Che never expressed much of an opinion on Perón's approach, but the search for a 'Third Position' struck a chord with his reading of Nehru's 1946 book *The*

Discovery of India. Both leaders were attempting to find a way out of the debilitating hold that the colonial powers had over countries that yearned for political and economic liberty. And both leaders saw that without economic freedom, political freedom meant very little.

On the Indian subcontinent the colonial power whose shackles had to be shaken free was Britain. In Argentina the economic power often lay in the hands of British companies, but also increasingly the Americans were coming to the fore. And it wasn't only in Argentina that the USA was gaining influence and power. All across South America, and especially in Central America, the US was imperialistically pursuing its own economic interests. The more Che read about and considered the situation, the more he came to see America as one of the twin evils holding Latin America both back and down. The other evil was the internal power structures and class-based interest groups of the countries themselves.

But while his analysis of regional politics may have been deepening, in many ways he behaved just like any other typical student. He cultivated the image of an outsider, and in a society where the sharp cut of a pair of trousers or a blazer were much admired among the young, he prided himself in looking permanently dishevelled.

While those around him favoured the 1950s fads of blue jeans, Italian shirts or British pullovers, Che would wear a once-white nylon shirt, now grey from overwashing, and a shapeless pair of trousers held up by a length of clothesline.

Despite his unconventional dress sense, his good looks and his social rebel posturing made him a very attractive young man. And he took full advantage of this as he would relentlessly pursue the seduction of many of the girls and women he met.

He was also perennially short of money and came up with strange schemes to raise cash. Once he hit on the idea of repackaging an agricultural locust insecticide and selling it as a cockroach killer for the home. He even went so far as to secure a patent for his product. But the scheme bit the dust when the 'factory' he set up at home caused him to fall ill. Another abandoned money spinner was buying shoes cheap at a wholesale auction, then selling them door to door. After this operation also folded Che salvaged two shoes of different colours and wore them as discordant footwear that just added to his unconventional look.

As well as needing the money that he hoped his aborted capitalist schemes would generate to support himself, he also needed it in order to help pay for food on the trips away from Buenos Aires that he had started to embark upon. Initially Che hitch-hiked, spending a couple of days at a time on his adventures. But before long he wanted to travel further, to spend longer away, to discover at first hand more of the country that he had been born into.

At the end of his third year in medical school, in January 1950, he set off on a motorised bicycle and headed towards Córdoba. In the six weeks, and 4,000 kilometres, that lay ahead of him he was to at last encounter the harsh realities of a country that was split between the imported culture of European settlers in which he had grown up and the often grinding poverty and crushed spirits of indigenous natives of the interior. He travelled among, talked to and shared meagre meals with lepers, prisoners, tramps and hospital inmates. And while his readings at university had given him an intellectual grasp of the often brutal mechanics of inequality his travels presented him with the real human consequences. All the while he knew that he was exploring this world of the dispossessed and marginalised from a position of privilege.

To try to help himself remember all that he saw, and to make sense of it, Che began the habit of keeping a daily diary. It would be a habit that stayed with him his entire life.

The Graduate

☆ ☆ ☆

TO RETURN TO CAMBRIDGE for his final year was a kind of relief. Although Cha never felt at ease in an environment that seemed to him dominated by long-haired and bare-footed students, and a communal living ethos totally at odds with his character, he did at least manage to create a lifestyle of his own. Weekends away shooting 'other people's pheasants' continued to be important. And in his new set of rooms he began to hold 'endless dinner parties in a crazy way!'. On top of all this he was increasingly involved in official duties and would sometimes be called upon to stand in for his mother.

He attended state banquets, he welcomed visiting royalty and heads of state, he ate at formal lunches and he walked beside his mother at the state opening of Parliament. Official visits outside Britain also began to feature heavily in his diary. One trip took him to Australia, Hong Kong and New Zealand. On another he found himself representing Britain at the opening of Expo 70 in Japan. Yet another had him stopping off in Canada before spending time in the United States of America.

It was in Washington during an Oval Office audience with President Nixon that Cha pushed the conversation away from small talk about polo and baseball into questions about Russia and China. Surprisingly, Cha even broached the subject of the queen visiting Moscow. Even more surprisingly, especially given the president's firm anti-Soviet stance and rhetoric, Nixon thought it would be a good idea. But then again he also considered his strategy in Cambodia a 'success'.

That Cha wanted to find out what the people he met thought about the key issues of the day clearly shows that his mind was an enquiring one. He was, by all accounts, a very good listener. Given that it had long been drummed into him that it would be extremely unwise to express himself on any issue that might be deemed controversial, it is revealing that he had such a thirst for knowledge. Indeed, about the only place where he felt he could share and explore his thoughts and opinions was in the letters he wrote, and in the journals he began to keep. Both were habits that have sustained him, and helped define himself to himself, all through his life.

In between all of this Charles also managed to study. He got a 2:2. He was the first heir to the throne to earn such a poor degree. But he was also the first heir to the throne to earn any degree. Given how disrupted his university life had been it was a pretty good achievement.

He left Cambridge as the sixties ended. In many ways he appeared to have remained largely untouched by the political turmoil and social upheaval of the decade. But, in retrospect, that is clearly a superficial analysis. Sometimes the seeds that are sown lie deep in the soil. And it takes a long time for the shoots to push their way to the surface.

Perhaps a true indication of just how radical an individual Cha really was as he came of age is revealed in a story he wrote around that time to entertain his younger siblings. One wet Wednesday, trapped within the cramped confines and experiencing the sobering hardships of life aboard the royal yacht *Britannia*, he created a deceptively simple fable to amuse the brothers he had affectionately dubbed 'Andyou' and 'Headwood'.

It was a tale set among the hills, glens, lochs and porridge bogs of his beloved Scotland. And many years later a version of it was published in Britain to raise money for charity. However, the version that the public had the chance to buy and read was but a sorry travesty of the original.

What follows is that original story. Nothing has been taken out. Nothing has been added. When you have finished reading it, and pondered its coded but clear message it will be easy for you to understand why the original was suppressed by powerful elements in both the Palace and in Her Majesty's Government.

Included with the text of the story are a selection of the original illustrations that Cha commissioned from

his close personal friend and fellow traveller Sir Huge
Cassock BOAC.

THE OLD GROUSE OF LOCHCUBAR

Cha Windsera

Illustrated by Sir Huge Cassock B.O.A.C.

Not all that long ago, when bairns were even smaller and people had especially hairy armpits, a wicked laird seized control of the beautiful land of Lochcubar.

All day, all night, and even on early closing Wednesdays, he smoked the vile cigarettes of exploitation and planned shoots to hunt down the gentle grouse that lived by the shores of the Loch.

When ever he smiled his evil-weeded smile his teeth were black with the nicotine of oppression and so the down-trodded grouse, squinting out from their humble heather bowers, fearfully dubbed him Bad Teeth Tar.

But as even the wee-est of babby grouse-lets knows, oppression is a kipper that curls up when you cook it. That's why the most subjugated of subjects will never lie flat for long.

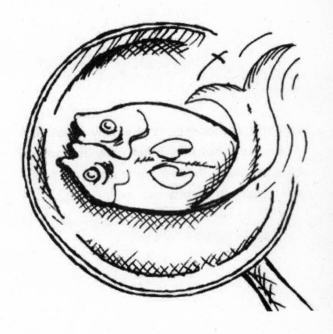

Soon the porridge of rebellion was not just being stirred, but salted too, by a true grouse of the people, with fire in his feathers, and steel (and a cigar) in his beak.

Fidel Groustro – for it was he – had long watched his beloved Lochcubar with despair (of binoculars) from his exile across the waters of the Loch and resolved to overthrow Bad Teeth Tar and all that he stood, sat and sometimes lay down for.

In a wicker and hide coracle so old and leaky that he nicknamed it 'Granma' Fidel set sail with eighty-two brave *grouspeneros*, provisioned with a sporran full of victuals and armed (or should that be winged?) with an ancient collection of rusting sgian dubhs.*

---

* Pronounced 'traditional Scottish daggers'.

For seven days and seven minutes the intrepid sailors braved the storms of the open Loch. But Fidel steadied their nerves, stiffened their resolve and generally blanched their blaeberries by making seven hour-long patriotic speeches, that always ended in the revolting Scottish cry of 'Hasta la victoria siempre, Jimmae!'

On the seventh day and the eighth minute of their expedition the band of brothers beached the sodden Granma in the Bay Of Haggii and leapt ashore. But they had gone awry. There were none of the haggis trees that they thought would give them cover. There was just a solitary hardy perennial shrub, laden with an early crop of Ayrshire middle back bacon (unsmoked). They had landed in the Bay of Pigs. And they had run straight into a ham bush.

From behind the ham bush leapt the beaters and the guns of a hunt that Bad Teeth Tar had arranged as a surprise welcome. A hail of shots rained down on the eighty-two brave *grous-peneros*. In a storm of moulting lead and flying feathers, as their comrades fell around them, despairing cries of 'Go back! Go Back!' were heard from the grousing grouse. But Fidel stood firm and cried out 'No bird surrenders here'.

Eighty-two had made landfall, but only twelve remained when the dishevelled and wearied covey of renegades regrouped in The Highlands above the Loch. Their weapons were all but gone, and their provisions numbered but half a squished tatty and a solitary, down at heel, neep.

But Fidel, the Glorious Twelfth survivor, was not the kind of *Lagopus lagopus* to get gloomy in the gloaming. Instead he drilled his comrades in first chimp, then baboon, and finally gorilla war. Constantly on the move, they hit and ran, harassed and embarrassed, and generally got right up the snooty hooties of Bad Teeth Tar's leaden-footed hunters. With each small victory they captured more of their enemy's guns. And the legend of 'The Red Grouse' grew.

In all that they did they cultivated the support of the oppressed grouse around them who grubbed a meagre living with the honest sweat of their brows. All Bad Teeth Tar could do was grind his teeth, and try to grind down these self-same grouse, accusing them of sheltering the rebels. Little wonder then that soon huge swathes of The Highlands flocked to Fidel's side and took refuge under his capacious wing.

Bad Teeth Tar struck back by arranging The Shoot of Ten Thousand Guns. But the *grouspeneros*, by now 300 strong, were no sitting ducks. They flew rings around their would-be executioners. The tide had turned, and the discontented chickens of the dictatorship were finally coming home to roost.

From his stronghold in The Highlands Fidel sent out a brace of rebel columns to advance on The Glens. One took the high road, one took the low road. And, hill by dale, valley by vale, The Glens welcomed them as conquering heroes. Bad Teeth Tar, seeing all was lost, fled Lochcubar for ever.

WHO DO YOU THINK YOU ARE KIDDING MR. TEETHTAR?

That night Fidel Groustro – The Old Grouse of Lochcubar – declared an end to all oppression. From now on all the grouse of this happy land would be free – and enjoy excellent health care provision. And the grateful grouses rejoiced long into the night in a joyous Grouse Ceilidh.*

The End.
Or is it just the beginning?

---

* Incidentally, the very next morning this Grouse Ceilidh went and married our distant relative Prince Rainallyear of Monacle.

As the 1970s dawned and the world headed off into a brave new decade that would see so many of the ideals of the sixties crash to earth the big question was, what should Cha do next?

'And suddenly that name, will never be the same again'

★ ★ ★

WHEN CHE RETURNED TO UNIVERSITY it was to begin his fourth year of studies. He was twenty-two years old. And his travels had opened his eyes to the harsh realities of a country where the poverty and exploitation of the masses supported and sustained the privileged lives of the elite.

Then something happened to Che that had never happened before. He fell in love. He fell in love with a girl called Maria. She was sixteen years old. She was beautiful. And she was the daughter of one of Córdoba's oldest and wealthiest families.

It was a family whose fortune was based on a lime quarry manned by workers who lived in a quasi-feudal village. A family who lived in a grand French-style château with grounds containing not one, but two polo fields. A family who even had a separate alcove at the church they attended so they would be spared the indignity of having to kneel at the same communion rail as the workers who laboured so hard through the week to build their fortune.

If you want proof that love is blind, then here it is. The girl Che had fallen for was an heiress to everything that he was beginning to question, and everything he was growing to despise.

Che had known Maria from his own time in Córdoba. When his family went back there to attend a wedding he discovered the little girl he remembered had grown into a stunning young woman. As soon as they met it was clear that she was as drawn to him as he was to her.

At first Maria's family accepted Che and the burgeoning romance. His nonconformity, while noted, was not seen as a great worry as they themselves had more than a fair share of colourful characters in their ranks and among their ancestors. And Maria was only sixteen; how serious could the relationship be?

During 1951 Che continued to break off from his studies and travel to see Maria back at her home in Córdoba. And before long, on these visits, he began to talk to Maria about marriage. He even went so far as to outline the honeymoon that he had planned with the two of them touring South America in a motor caravan.

When word of these discussions reached Maria's parents the attitude towards Che began to change. Where he was tolerated before he now found himself encountering fierce opposition. His opinions, in the past indulged as amusing, now came to be seen as provocatively confrontational. And the disapproval he encountered only goaded Che into being more outrageous. The situation came to a head during a family meal where the discussion centred on Winston Churchill, whom Maria's family thought of as a hero. When he had heard enough Che joined in by deriding Britain's wartime leader as nothing but a 'ratpack politician'. Maria's father walked out in disgust.

Despite all this the relationship between Che and Maria continued. But it had to be conducted clandestinely. And it continued, in letter form at least, when at the end of 1950 Che took a temporary job aboard an oil tanker as a ship's 'doctor'.

When he wasn't attending to his duties, or writing to Maria, he wrote a melodramatic autobiographical essay entitled 'Anguish (That's Right)'. It is a piece shot through with loneliness, frustrated emotions about Maria, and the longing to break free from society's constraints. It starts with a quote from Ibsen:

Education is the capacity to confront the
situations posed by life,

and ends with the sentiment:

To make a sterile sacrifice that does nothing to
raise up a new life: that is anguish.

When he finished his stint on the tanker he went back to medical school. He was twenty-three and a further two years of study lay ahead of him before he would qualify. His love affair with Maria, who was still only seventeen, appeared to be going nowhere as her parents had entrenched their opposition to the potential union. All of which made his friend Alberto Granado's suggestion that he join him in a long dreamt-of trip around South America all the more appealing.

They were to travel on a vintage 500cc Norton motorcycle that they nicknamed 'la Poderosa' – 'the Powerful One'. And they aimed to see South America in all its grandeur, and all its grimness. It was to be the trip that Che was later to write up in his *Motorcycle Diaries*.

Che and Alberto set out on 4 January 1952. They travelled along the Atlantic coast and first aimed for the seaside resort of Miramar. Maria was holidaying there and Che wanted to say goodbye before he set off. So that she would remember him as he travelled he carried on the back of the Norton a present for her. It was small, wriggling puppy. When she asked him what it was called he told her that its name was the English phrase 'Come-back'.

With that he and Alberto rode off into the sunset.

'You can sail the Seven Seas ...'

☆ ☆ ☆

THE NEXT STAGE in Cha's life was to enter service in
the armed forces. For a leader of a revolution military
experience is invaluable. Physical prowess is valued.
Courage is expected. The ability to succeed in the face
of adversity is prized. And the theory and practice of
conflict become subjects that are studied and internal-
ised. Above all else the serviceman gets to understand
that discipline, both personal and in those around him,
is vital when he enters a battle with the odds stacked
against him. (Those were the days.) Equally important
for a leader who craves not only action, but thought
too, is the fact that close-up experience of conventional military methods can't help but reveal that, no
matter how technically proficient those methods are,
they do have their limitations. Put more succinctly, it's
easier to think outside the box if you know how the
box is constructed in the first place.

The choice of service was relatively simple. Cha's
father had been an impressive Royal Navy officer who
had been forced to put his career on hold when he
had married. Equally importantly Mountbatten, who

was rapidly becoming Cha's true mentor, had been an almost indecently distinguished naval top banana. Both men championed the Royal Navy. Indeed so keen were they in forwarding the cause of the Senior Service that the Christmas after Cha left Cambridge, while his mother's speech was on the telly and everyone was in danger of nodding off on the sofa, the duo performed an impromptu recital of 'In The Navy' before roping in the Queen Mother to lead a somewhat risqué version of 'Sailing'.

Initially Cha signed up for three years. After that he would be allowed to decide whether to extend his tour of duty.

Before he enrolled at the Royal Naval College at Dartmouth he did four months with the RAF learning to fly jets. He had already mastered propeller planes during his second year at university. On 31 March 1971 he did his first solo flight in a Jet Provost. Soon after that he learned to parachute jump. For many reasons this was thought to be a good idea.

When Cha entered Dartmouth he found that after the relative freedom of university life it was an environment depressingly reminiscent of being back at school. Demeaning and baffling in equal measure, the college's real aim was to drum into its inmates the rudiments of seamanship and naval technology, traditions and customs. For Cha the experience was even more intense as he was being fast-tracked and the normal twelve-week course was compressed into only six. By all accounts he did reasonably well, but he found military technology hard to grasp and navigation a constant challenge. A contemporary of his remembers his 'endearing vagueness' whilst his self-deprecating sense of humour and modesty put his fellow trainees at ease.

He joined his first ship, HMS *Norfolk*, in the Mediterranean on 5 November 1971. Guy Fawkes night. All across Britain people would be remembering a man who had tried to blow up the Houses of Parliament. His commanding officer was a Captain Cook. And Captain Cook was the same name as the man who had, two centuries earlier, sailed off into the unknown and discovered a new world* before returning to found the old world's first travel agency.

As Cha's naval career progressed he was still often beset by self-doubt. He was also constantly aware that everything he ever did was being closely scrutinised. And if it wasn't enough that his elders and betters back at the Palace and the top brass at Admiralty House were keeping an eye on him, there was also the unwelcome attentions of the press to contend with. In a media-saturated world that had boomed since the late sixties, and a press environment that was heading inexorably towards tabloidifying circulation wars, Cha's progress was a storyline that was just too good to leave alone for long.

---

* Just how 'new' a new world can be when there are already people living there is a question that imperialistic empires have never really come to terms with.

So keen were the press to discover as much as they could about the man who would one day be king that, when he embarked on a stint aboard the £30-million nuclear submarine HMS *Churchill*, one newspaper hired a trained dolphin with a camera strapped to its snout to trail the boat and get pictures. Unfortunately for the newspaper the navy got wind of the scheme and sent one of their most attractive female SBS-trained dolphins to lure the spy away in a classic 'honeypot' operation. When the editor of the newspaper got the pictures back he soon realised that they were totally inappropriate for use in a mass-market daily. (The female dolphin was flat-chested.)

As well as learning how to fly a submarine the Prince took courses in missile warfare, gunnery, macramé, how to lead a riot squad and what to do should a man fall overboard. (Rescue him, apparently, which is reassuring.)

Although being a naval officer did not come easily to him, he persevered and soon developed a reputation for being sympathetic to the lot of the 'other ranks' below deck. He came to see them, somewhat clicheingly, as 'the salt of the earth'. (Why he did not see them as the more appropriate and far less clichey 'salt of the sea' is not recorded.)

One part of naval life he did excel at was in the keeping of a journal, an age-old naval tradition. His effort was judged by one superior as the best he had ever read, but another did point out that it contained 'too many non-nautical terms'. Apparently he used the somewhat alarming phrase 'he's fallen in the water' a little too often for comfort.

As Cha charted his course from one ship to the next he would occasionally find himself wheeled out to fly the flag at official functions. On the whole he found such situations a chore. The only way to get through them was to make sure the whole thing was meticulously planned. If this was done, the endless round of shaking hands, small talk and long drawn-out meals, became less of an ordeal.

What such occasions did highlight, however, was Cha's strange dual role. He was in some respects nothing more than a junior naval officer learning his trade. But he was also heir to the throne. And that too, as he had long since known, was a trade that had to be learned. This duality that he existed within was just one aspect of a character that was increasingly coming to be defined by a series of paradoxes.

He was insecure, but could be wilful. He was reticent, but was becoming opinionated. He was gentle, but had an impassioned side to him. He was reflective, but could leap in impulsively. And he believed in hierarchy, but undercut it with an irreverent, anarchic sense of humour. On top of all that some days he wore Y-fronts and on others boxer shorts. (And on days when he was feeling particularly insecure, or had to do a navigation test, he would wear both.)

The fact that he was expected to be the smiling face of Britain from Honolulu to Hollywood, from the Caribbean to Colombia, from Wick to Warminster, was a constant reminder of the life that lay ahead of him. So little free time did he have that any single day during which he wasn't boxed in by naval or royal duties was one to be cherished. He especially valued any time he could spend in the company of his uncle Mountbatten, who was probably the only person to whom he felt he could open up. But even on these occasions there always lurked behind most conversations the idea of duty.

In the end Charles decided to extend his period of service in the navy to five years. As time went by he did grow in confidence. And although his views on the world were rarely sought they were forming and being placed in a framework of his own. He even started to develop a public image, courtesy of the press, as a bit of an 'action man'.

He left the navy in December 1976, having commanded the coastal minehunter HMS *Bronington* for nine months. He still couldn't navigate a ship. Whether he could navigate himself in the stormy waters that lay ahead was a completely different question.

But, undoubtedly, he had gained the trust and affection of his crew. Indeed, on the night before his departure the under-rehearsed and largely tone deaf 'Oily Chart Company' performed a comic light opera in the mess room for him as a farewell tribute. It was written by Midshipman Gilbert O'Sullivan and entitled *HMS Metaphor*. The best, and most pertinent, song in the show was called 'When I Was A Lad':

The Prince:	When I was a lad I served my time My only duty was to wait in line I learned how monarchy was handed down And I polished up the jewels on the family crown
The Crew:	He polished up the jewels on the family crown
Prince:	I polished up the jewels so carefully And now I am a captain in my mum's navy
Crew:	He polished up the jewels so carefully And now he is a captain in his mum's navy
Prince:	I went to school and university Discovering what my role should be My life was set I had no choice I practised my wave and my speaking voice
Crew:	He practised his wave and his speaking voice
Prince:	I practised my wave so regally And now I am a captain in my mum's navy
Crew:	He practised his wave so regally And now he is a captain in his mum's navy

Prince: After three years at Cambridge I went to
sea
I went to see if it would suit me
I learned how to fly and parachute jump
But navigation just gave me the hump

Crew: But navigation just gave him the hump

Prince: At navigation I was skill free
And now I am a captain in my mum's
navy

Crew: At navigation he was skill free
And now he is a captain in his mum's
navy

Prince: Off the shores of Britain I float around
And try my best not to run aground
I search for mines assiduously
But in so many ways I'm all at sea

Crew: But in so many ways he's all at sea

Prince: In so many ways I'm all at sea
And I am a captain in my mum's navy

Crew: In so many ways he's all at sea
And he is a captain in his mum's navy

Prince: I've learned to command but I'm always
vexed
The really big question is what comes next
When I get out my role is just to wait
And the more I think about it it starts to
grate

Crew:	The more he thinks about it it starts to grate
Prince:	The more I think about it it starts to grate Perhaps I'm just a deckhand on the Ship of State
Crew:	The more he thinks about it it starts to grate Perhaps he's just a deckhand on the Ship of State
Prince:	I've broken the rhyme scheme in the last verse Maybe that's the answer to the fears I nurse To find my own role I must break free This prince must decide what to be or not to be
Crew:	This prince must decide what to be or not to be
Prince:	This prince must decide what to be or not to be If I'm ever to be captain of my own navy
Crew:	This prince must decide what to be or not to be If he's ever to be captain of his own navy!

The Heart of the Darkness

★ ★ ★

BEFORE CHE AND ALBERTO had got very far the younger man succumbed to a fever. As a result Che was laid up in hospital for several days. Time, no doubt, to contemplate what lay ahead, and ponder on what he had left behind. Once recovered the pair boarded the Norton again and rode off towards the lake district that bordered Chile on the eastern slopes of the Andean cordillera. It was there that Che received a letter from Maria.

Maria, still only seventeen, broke the news to Che that she was not going to wait for him. Che was devastated: 'I read and reread the incredible letter. Just like that, all (my) dreams ... came crashing down ...'

Apparently Maria had been seeing someone else. So now Che, his journey with Alberto barely begun, had to face the fact that the far more significant journey he had hoped to return to was over.

At least the road that lay ahead would take his mind off things. And the break in the relationship meant that whatever he faced he would do so free of all ties. Che and Alberto crossed the border into Chile aboard a leaky cargo barge where they worked their passage by manning the bilge pumps.

In Chile Che hit on a plan to give themselves much needed credentials that would act as introductions on their journey. He and Alberto rode up to the offices of a local newspaper and presented themselves as 'leprosy experts' with 'previous research in neighbouring countries' . The newspaper, with no reason to doubt them, and no way of checking their credentials, duly reprinted their story in an article headlined 'Two Argentine Experts in Leprology Travel South America on Motorcycle'.

Alberto had, in fact, worked temporarily in a leper colony, and Che had visited him there, but to describe themselves as 'experts' was pushing it rather. However, the printed article, carefully cut out and kept as a reference, gave them some apparently bona fide credentials that would prove invaluable on their travels. It also showed that they were fully willing and able to duck and dive with the best of them in order to go on their way.

But as well as opening doors, helping them gain trust and even providing beds in hospitals along the way, their fake credentials meant they were sometimes called upon to act as doctors. In one bar where the owner had taken them in Che was asked to see if he could do anything for one of the establishment's clients, an old servant woman who had serious heart problems and asthma. As soon he examined her Che knew there was nothing he could do. She was dying.

The meeting made a deep impression on Che. If his readings at university had given him an intellectual understanding of the nature of poverty, here, in a small room that smelled of 'concentrated sweat and dirty feet', was the ugly reality:

> There, in the final moments of people whose
> farthest horizon is always tomorrow, one sees the
> tragedy that enfolds the lives of the proletariat
> throughout the whole world; in those dying
> eyes there is a submissive apology and also,
> frequently, a desperate plea for consolation that
> is lost in the void, just as their body will be lost
> in the magnitude of misery surrounding us. How
> long this order of things based on an absurd
> sense of caste will continue is not within my
> means to answer, but it is time that those who
> govern dedicate less time to propagandizing the
> compassion of their regimes and more money,
> much more money, sponsoring works of social
> utility.

Further cause for thought came when the two travellers made a point of visiting the Chuquicamata copper mine. It was the largest open-cast mine in the world and the mainstay of Chile's economy. Being US owned and run it was also the focus of heated political debate on the subject of the foreign domination of the economy through monopolistic companies over which the Chilean people had no real control or influence.

Naturally many Chileans argued for the nationalisation of the mines, and in response the US companies, with the help of the US government, pushed for the break-up of the mining unions and the outlawing of the Communist Party of Chile.

But once again it was when Che encountered the true human face of such a conflict that the rhetoric of both sides was given real meaning.

While waiting in a desert for a lift halfway to the mine he and Alberto met a marooned couple. The husband was a striking miner recently released from prison. His comrades had disappeared and he assumed that they had been murdered. And as a member of the Chilean Communist Party he couldn't find work. His only option was to head to the sulphur mines where working conditions were so bad they were grateful to hire anyone who turned up. No questions asked. Having left their children with a neighbour, that's where he and his wife were heading.

By the light of the single candle which illuminated us ... the contracted features of the worker gave off a mysterious and tragic air ... The couple, frozen stiff in the desert night, hugging one another, were a live representation of the proletariat of any part of the world. They didn't even have a miserable blanket to cover themselves, so we gave them one of ours, and with the other Alberto and I covered ourselves as best we could. It was one of the times when I felt the most cold, but it was also the time when I felt a little more in fraternity with this, for me, strange human species.

Given all this it is hardly surprising that he saw his eventual visit to the copper mine, with its appalling working conditions, in political terms. He even regarded the as yet untouched mountains around Chuquicamata as further examples of the 'exploited proletariat' just waiting for 'the arid arms of the mechanical shovels that devour their entrails, with their obligatory condiments of human lives'.

After Chile Che and Alberto crossed over into Peru and found themselves in the Indian town of Tarata. Here elements of the racism that lay so close to the surface in much of South America, and had defined so much of its last 400 years of history, became clearly illustrated in their encounters with the 'beaten race':

> (They watch) us pass through the streets of the town. Their stares are tame, almost fearful, and completely indifferent to the outside world. Some give the impression that they live because it is a habit they can't shake off.

Che and Alberto also took time to visit the ancient ruins of the Inca capital at Cuzco. Here Che's loathing for the 'Yankee masters' of Chile's mines was matched by his disgust for American tourists whom he characterised as 'blonde, camera-toting, sport-shirted correspondents from another world' who 'visit the ruins and then return, without giving any importance to anything else'.

After four months of travelling they arrived in Lima, the capital of Peru. There they were taken in and welcomed by a leading leprosy expert called Dr Hugo Pesce. He was a man both travellers soon came to respect greatly. Pesce was not only an expert leprologist, and a university lecturer, but also a member of the Peruvian Communist Party. And he was a disciple of the Peruvian Marxist philosopher Mariátegui, who had advocated the revolutionary potential of the local Latin American Indians. How important Pesce was in Che's development can easily be gauged by the inscription Che wrote in the copy of his book *Guerrilla Warfare* that he sent to him many years later:

> To Doctor Hugo Pesce: who, without knowing
> it perhaps, provoked a great change in my
> attitude towards life and society, with the same
> adventurous spirit as always, but channelled
> towards goals more harmonious with the needs of
> America.

In brief, Che had discovered in Dr Hugo an outstanding man of medicine who was not only dedicating his life to both intellectually and practically fighting the diseases of the body, but also doing the same for the diseases of society.

Little wonder, then, that the young Che respectfully referred to the older doctor as 'el Maestro'.

No future?

☆ ☆ ☆

LEAVING THE NAVY had been the easy part. But an heir to the throne in a demob suit is not the easiest person to find employment for down at the Job Centre. Especially in a Britain where unemployment seemed to be inexorably on the rise. It was a dilemma that Cha himself was completely aware of, as a speech he made on a return trip to Cambridge University clearly shows:

> My great problem in life is that I do not really
> know what my role is. At the moment I do not
> have one. But somehow I must find one.

While the people who for so long had chosen his path for him debated where he should head, Cha started developing his own ideas. He realised that the sanitised versions of reality he encountered on official visits gave a ludicrously circumscribed view of whatever he was being pointed at. Instead he suggested that rather than spending three hours at a factory, smiling at conveyor belts and shaking hands, maybe he should spend three days on site to really discover how the place worked. Or three days on a trawler. Or on a farm.

He also identified the need to visit areas of Britain's inner cities where immigrants lived as a way of showing them encouragement and acceptance. In a time when race relations were always an issue, the National Front was gaining support and the relationship between young black people and the police was on the verge of boiling over, Cha's desires were far-sighted. But they were also worrying for an establishment who would much rather have had him do something far less controversial. The Governorship of Australia was mooted. As was involvement in the workings of the National Economic Development Office.

But Cha wanted to be far more hands on. He wanted to find a way of tackling the problems he saw burgeoning in Britain in the second half of the seventies. And he was particularly drawn to the problems faced by the young and disadvantaged. Somewhat bizarrely, especially as he spent a large part of his time there being beaten up, he initially drew inspiration from Gordonstoun school. He suggested that part-time volunteer services would give the young confidence and the pride of achievement.

Before long this somewhat do-goody, top-down approach to helping the young had evolved into a fledgling, if loosely structured, organisation focused on people between fifteen and twenty five who were 'alienated or rejected' or 'aimless and lacking in purpose' and unable to use conventional educational routes to achieve 'economic and personal autonomy'. It would provide small grants to small groups to enable them to set up self-help schemes. In short it aimed to find the young people in society who were marginalised and on the scrap heap, had the balls to do something about it, but just needed a little initial support.

For all these reasons Cha somewhat wittily christened it the Prince's Truss.

Every revolutionary has to fight a first battle somewhere. For Cha setting up the Prince's Truss would be just such a struggle. Getting the Truss off the ground meant having to outmanoeuvre the forces of conservatism that naturally held sway in the Palace hierarchy. Cha also found himself up against senior royal advisers who often had been in positions of influence since he was a child, and tended to view him as being still too young and inexperienced to be taken seriously.

But the trainee revolutionary was determined. While he was not in position as yet to storm the Palace gates, he was clever and agile enough to, metaphorically, clamber over the back wall and jimmy open a window. To this end he got three pilot schemes up and running. When they succeeded he ploughed forward, overriding all opposition with an implacable determination that came as a revelation to many. And when the fledgling scheme was in danger of being strangled at birth by insolvency he financed the venture by paying into its coffers a £4,000 cheque he had received for an American television interview about George III.

However, the detailed work required to be the

head of an organisation that had the ambitions that the Prince's Truss had was something that was, as yet, beyond him. He was still a leader driven more by inspiration than perspiration. When faced with setbacks he could react with petulance. When faced with administrative necessities he could not long disguise his lack of concentration. Clearly, in endeavouring to create the Prince's Truss Cha had launched his first struggle with the authorities only to find that the struggle within himself was one he still had to deal with.

Despite all this the Truss was officially opened in 1976. It was a year when a seemingly endless drought hit Britain and dried up the rivers and reservoirs. A year when industrial unrest rumbled on unabated. And a year when, almost as a presage of the turmoil that was to come, the Notting Hill Carnival erupted into rioting.

In truth there was very little that Cha could do to help prevent the anomie that lay ahead. But at least he was aware of what was happening. And concerned about it. And through the humble beginnings of the Prince's Truss he had switched the message from one of the well-meaning, hand-wringing, platitudes that 'Something must be done' to the more practical 'What can I do?'

Some of the first young people that the Prince's Truss helped ran a small clothes-retailing operation in a run-down part of inner-city Chelsea. They were a couple called Malcolm and Vivienne. In many ways they were the embodiment of just the kind of individuals that

Cha had envisaged that his Truss could support. The fast-talking Malcolm and the quieter Vivienne sold nostalgically Teddy-boyish clothes to the very dispossessed youth that Cha had began to care about so dearly. When Cha first met these two 'characters' he was very taken with the souped-up Edwardian Englishness of the designs he was shown. But as it turns out Vivienne was equally appreciative of what he was wearing.

That day Cha was just back from a trip to Scotland and so he was still kitted out in a tartan kilt and a sporran. The Truss put money into the fledgling clothing venture and with this much-needed financial support Malcolm and Vivienne put together a new collection of clothing that featured lots of tartan and their own radically redesigned version of the kilt. Within a very short space of time the clothes were making waves and Malcolm was selling out. Without the support of the Truss none of this would have been possible.

In a subsequent meeting Cha let slip that he was of the opinion that with the Silver Jubilee coming up maybe it was time that most traditional of celebrations – the national anthem – was updated. What was needed, said Cha, was something that young people could really 'relate to' and maybe even dance some kind of 'jig' to.

Malcolm was at first sceptical, saying that the national anthem was an 'icon' that shouldn't be desecrated by tampering. But when Cha showed him the full lyrics of 'God Save the Queen' he began to see why

Cha was so uneasy about the values expressed by the words:

God save our gracious Queen
Long live our noble Queen
God save the Queen
Send her victorious
Happy and Glorious
Long to reign over us
God save the Queen

O Lord, our God, arise
Scatter thine enemies
And make them fall
Confound their politics
Frustrate their knavish tricks
On thee our hopes we fix
God save us all

Thy choicest gifts in store
On her be please to pour
Long may she reign
May she defend our laws
And ever give us cause
To sing with heart and voice
God save the Queen

Cha was also somewhat disappointed by a poem that the Poet Laureate Sir John Betjeman had composed to celebrate the Silver Jubilee. The poem began:

In days of disillusion,
However low we've been
To fire us and inspire us
God gave to us our Queen

She acceded, young and dutiful
To her much-loved father's throne;
Serene and kind and beautiful,
She holds us as her own.

Addressing Malcolm's concerns directly, Cha went on to say that what he wanted wasn't a song that was a deferential 'icon', but one instead that made the young people feel 'I can'.

Malcolm went away from the meeting deep in thought. A few months later he returned with a white-label seven-inch disc that he played to Cha. Before he let the music play he explained to Cha that in order to get a true feel for the record he needed to dance to it. Malcolm showed him a set of intricate steps based on the Morris dance classic 'Strip The Willow', but it proved far too complicated for Cha to follow. He said he'd rather improvise something himself and, going with the thrashing beat of the music, hit on the idea of just bouncing up and down on the spot.

It was, he explained, an egalitarian dance that anyone could do, so it wouldn't exclude any of the youth that society seemed only too eager to deem as being surplus to requirements.

The record was by a group called the Sex Pistols and

while Cha loved its energy and thrashing about to it in an improvised dance that his grandmother (who came into the room to see what all the racket was) dubbed pogoing, it was at first glance the anti-monarchist lyrics that resonated deepest with him.*

When Malcolm told Cha that he was having trouble getting the record put out by the large establishment record company that they had signed to Cha could only sympathise. When he was setting up the Prince's Truss he too had his own experience of the stifling conservative conformity that the establishment would habitually use to smother any effort to change things. In effect, he was saying that he knew just what it was to feel like a 'flower(s) in the dustbin'. Admittedly his particular dustbin was an especially well-appointed one, but the feeling of having your talents wasted, and the conviction that you are being marginalised, isn't one that just the dispossessed encounter.

As ever, Cha tried to come up with a practical way of helping Malcolm in his dispute with the record company. He advised him to provoke the company into firing the group, then once they were free of their commitments they could sign to a more radical label. He even suggested that the pickle magnate Richard Branston's Vergin' Records might be just the publicity hungry, media savvy bunch of opportunists to get in touch with. Malcolm wasn't convinced, but said he'd give them a try.

---

* And they are lyrics that are well worth looking up on the internet.

Seeing that the erstwhile music Svengali was still a tad down in the dumps as he left, Cha even pressed into his hand a parting gift to cheer him up. It was a portrait of his mother that Cha suggested could be used as the cover of the single. As he was handing the picture over it snagged on the corner of a half-eaten macaroon and ripped. Luckily Cha's grandmother, who was still in the room, managed to repair the tear with a safety pin that she had in her handbag.

Unfortunately, before the record ever came out Cha and Malcolm fell out. The essential problem was that Malcolm began to deny Cha's involvement in the group. Soon Malcolm was putting it around that he, and he alone, was the genius behind the Sex Pistols. Even the people in the group itself were, allegedly, merely puppets who did little more than wear the clothes they were given, sell the attitude they were instructed in, and mouth the words of their master. When Cha got to hear of this it gave him just another point on which to identify with the boys in the band, as this was exactly the same situation that he had been in for so many years. Subsequently he rang the lead singer of the group to express his support for them and characterised their manager's attitude as 'pretty vacant'.

If the struggle to set up the Prince's Truss was Cha's first rebellion, his next one was an altogether quieter and more introspective affair. In the late seventies the man who would one day be the head of that most conservative of organisations the Church of England embarked on a journey of spiritual inquiry that would take him far away from 'More tea, vicar?' and much closer to 'More mescal, shaman?'

His interest in religion had been present from his days at school, and had begun to widen out while he was at university. In the navy opportunities for pursuing matters spiritual were decidedly limited. Since coming out, however, he had plenty of time, and the temperament, to ponder the 'meaning of it all'.

No doubt just as he found the conventions, traditions and strictures of the more conservative elements of the royal court stifling, he also found the Church of England equally limiting. Cha was drawn to the subject of mysticism and intrigued by questions of the relationship between the self and the human soul. If such interests put him at odds with the conservative organised Church, it also put him at odds with the prevailing intellectual climate that worshipped at the altar of scientific rationalism.

Cha was drawn to the writings of Jung, which have it that the purpose of life is the integration of the self and that the real journey we are all embarked on is the one towards self-discovery. Cha's search for 'an inner world of truth' led him to read about, consider and explore the ancient religions of the East, which still revered and observed the mystical elements he found so patently lacking in a C of E Sunday service.

He was particularly intrigued by a book called *The Path of the Masters*, which was a guide to the spiritual wisdom of the Eastern gurus. Within this tome was one concept that struck a most harmonious chord with him. This was the idea that religious experience was an individual sensation, free of creed and dogma, but compatible with all faiths. Given that when he eventually inherited the throne he would become head of a church encrusted with both creed and dogma, it was a radical sentiment to identify with. Follow such a sentiment through to its logical conclusion and even the very oaths he would swear at his coronation would have to be rewritten. He could no longer be 'Defender of the Faith' and would only really be comfortable with 'Defender of Faith'.

Ten years after he was at university in the swinging sixties, Cha was, in part at least, turning decidedly hippyish. But as there was no one around to sell him any marijuana, and cheesecloth shirts don't really go with double-breasted suits, his retreat into a mystical world was largely a private one. One of its few outward expressions was Cha's burgeoning friendship with Laurens Hertz van Rental.

Hertz van Rental was a white South African writer, explorer, mystic and storyteller. He was famous for retelling the ancient legends of the bushmen of the Kalahari. He wrote a book called *The Lost World of the Kalahari* which was later turned into a television series that mesmerised millions of viewers. Cha was much taken with Hertz van Rental's notion that 'one should be outward bound the inward way' and that 'we have abolished superstition of the heart only to install a superstition of the intellect in its place'. And his own experience of the landscape around Balmoral meant he could readily relate to the idea that the land was, somehow, sacred.

Hertz van Rental was also an egotistical self-publicist who could see the commercial and social value in his close association with the heir to the British throne. Hence his assertion that he was the last man alive capable of passing on the 'meaning' of the Kalahari desert and that the best way to do that would be to take Cha with him on a seven-week journey through the wilderness with a BBC film crew in tow. In the end, for various reasons, the trip was cut down to five days in Kenya without the cameras.

Hertz van Rental talked to Cha about Jung, the importance of dreams and the idea of the collective unconscious, and introduced to him the recurrent ancient notion of the 'Wise Old Man' or guru who acted as a guide and offered insight into the world based on wisdom and not just knowledge. He even went so far as to imply that Cha had subconsciously conjured up such a figure for himself in the children's story that he had written for his younger siblings years before.

A Note in the Margin

★ ★ ★

WHEN CHE RETURNED to Buenos Aires from the trip with Alberto he was a changed man. As he wrote up what came to be called *The Motorcycle Diaries* he recorded that, 'The person who wrote these notes died upon stepping once again onto Argentine soil.' And he went on to say, 'I am not I; at least I am not the same as I was before.'

Then, in a coda to the main narrative of the story of his trip, Che writes of an encounter of which his travelling companion has no recollection. And given the almost mystical description of the meeting there is a strong case for arguing that the encounter was a fictional device that allowed Che to crystallise the change he had gone through and also mark out the path ahead that he had chosen to walk along:

The stars drew light across the night sky in that
little mountain village, and the silence and the
cold made the darkness vanish away. It was – I
don't know how to explain it – as if everything
solid melted away into the ether, eliminating all

individuality and absorbing us, rigid, into the immense darkness.

The man's face was indistinct in the shadows; I could only see what seemed like the spark of his eyes.

Che went on to describe how, although he had heard the arguments before from 'many different people', they had never made an impression. He then reports the mysterious older man who had escaped the 'knife of dogmatism' in Europe and 'wandered from country to country, gathering thousands of adventures' as saying:

The future belongs to the people, and gradually, or in one strike, they will take power, here and in every country. The terrible thing is, the people need to be educated, and this they cannot do before taking power, only after.

I also know ... that you will die with a clenched fist and a tense jaw, the epitome of hatred and struggle, because you are not a symbol ... but a genuine member of the society to be destroyed.

Che's account of his reaction to this speech is undoubtedly drenched in hyperbole, but its passion is hard to deny. And its prophetic nature is uncanny:

The night, folding in at contact with his words, overtook me again, enveloping me within it ... I knew that when the great guiding spirit cleaves humanity into two antagonistic halves, I would be with the people. I know this, I see it printed in the night sky that I, eclectic dissembler of doctrine and psychoanalyst of dogma, howling like one possessed, will assault the barricades or the trenches, will take my bloodstained weapon and, consumed with fury, slaughter any enemy who falls into my hands. And I see, as if a great exhaustion smothers this fresh exaltation, I see myself, immolated in the genuine revolution, the great equalizer of individual will, proclaiming the ultimate *mea culpa*. I feel my nostrils dilate, savouring the acrid smell of gunpowder and blood, of the enemy's death; I steel my body, ready to do battle, and prepare to be a sacred space within which the bestial howl of the triumphant proletariat can resound with new energy and new hope.

So Che was no longer looking for a role for himself. What's truly remarkable is that he had, at twenty-five years of age, already mapped out how his movie would end.

Precious Moments

☆ ☆ ☆

IF CHA BOUGHT INTO the concept of the Wise Old Man it is hardly surprising. All his life he had had the need for just such a guide. Unfortunately, because of the difference in temperament and the emotional distance between them, his own father never comfortably fulfilled such a role. Not that his father didn't love him, it is more that his father didn't really understand him, or what he needed. Throw in the fact that his mother lived a life where her attention was often and constantly demanded by the affairs of state and it's easy to see why Cha grew up slightly adrift.

No doubt Laurens Hertz van Rental recognised this state of mind in the still, in many ways, young man that he tried to take under his wing. But if Hertz van Rental had cast himself as the guru, objectively speaking that role really belonged to Mountbatten.

Mountbatten had long been the one person that Cha could open up to and truly say what he felt, what he feared and what he dreamt of. Over the years Cha had come to know that in response he would get support, constructive criticism, advice and both love and respect. In return he loved, respected and admired the older man. In an attempt to accord his feelings the status that he felt they deserved he took to calling Mountbatten 'honorary grandfather'.

The support he gained from the older man took many forms and was constant over many years. When he had been a boy carefully selected presents, like a much longed-for bicycle, had been a tangible expression of love. As he grew up Cha found time in Mountbatten's company, and especially out in the landscape of Broadlands, both an escape and an adventure that he valued above almost anything else that he did. Even as a man heading towards his thirties, when he talked of his growing fascination with spirituality Mountbatten, though probably somewhat bemused by the enthusiasm, found a way to be positive about it, telling him that 'the great thing is to have some inspiration to cling to'.

In a world where his life from the very moment of his birth had been one hedged in by expectation and pored over, analysed and advised every step of the way, often by people with ulterior motives that were far from transparent, to have someone he could regard as 100 per cent on his side was invaluable.

One area that Cha definitely needed advice on was women. And Mountbatten was probably the only one who could give it. More importantly, he was also probably the only person Cha would feel comfortable listening to. The big problem was that anyone Cha got involved with would immediately be considered and evaluated by others, both privately and publicly, for 'queen potential'. Given that Cha was in essence a private, often socially ill at ease, young man, the prospect of having even the most innocent of adolescent encounters subjected to intrusive scrutiny was a far from alluring one.

Right from an early age Cha had the concept of duty drilled into him. A huge part of that duty was to marry and produce an heir. It was a concept which was a particularly well-honed Damoclesian sword to be hanging over every fumble in the bushes.

Mountbatten's response was to provide not only advice that fully understood Cha's unique predicament, but also practical help. For example, by giving Cha the run of Broadlands, if there were to be any 'carry-on behind the carriage sheds' at least the carriage sheds in question would be out of the prying sight of both the press and royal courtiers.

As for the advice, it was forthright, had the Prince's best interest at heart, but undoubtedly had its roots in a different age:

> I believe, in a case like yours, that a man should
> sow his wild oats and have as many affairs as he
> can before settling down. But for a wife he should
> choose a suitable and a sweet-charactered girl
> before she meets anyone else she might fall for.

The first woman Cha was really drawn to was Camilla Shand. They met in the late autumn of 1972 and it was soon evident that they had much in common. A big part of it was a shared sense of humour. She also fitted in to country life and, most important of all, made Cha feel at ease.

Unfortunately when they met Cha was in the navy. And come the new year he would have to fly out to the Caribbean to join his ship. Despite the briefness of their growing friendship it has been suggested that Cha was close to asking her to marry him. And in time he may well have done so. (Well, in time he did, but you know what I mean.) But time is precisely what the fledgling relationship did not have. That's because although Camilla fulfilled one part of Mountbatten's prospectus for a potential wife, she lacked another criterion. Before she had met Cha she had already been involved with someone else. And while Cha was serving with the navy in Antigua, barely six months after he and Camilla met, he learned that she had accepted a proposal of marriage from Andrew Parker Bowles.

Within a year Cha had become a big fan of The Three Degrees. A group whose biggest hit started off 'hoo-woo, haa-ah' followed by 'haa-ah, hoo-woo', then went on to heart-rendingly explore the sentiment of its oh-so painful title 'when will I see you again?'

As time went on it became apparent that Mountbatten wasn't just happy to provide Cha with advice on matters of the heart, and a private romantic setting to pursue affairs. He also thought he had found the person perfect to be Cha's wife. The person in question being his granddaughter Amanda Knatchbull. Over the course of the five years following 1974 he did whatever he could to steer the two youngsters, whom he loved dearly, closer and closer together. No doubt influenced by his mentor, Cha had even tentatively broached the subject of a possible marriage with Amanda's mother as early as 1974. Sensibly she said he shouldn't raise the subject with Amanda as she was still only sixteen. It was advice that probably relieved Cha greatly.

Nevertheless, between 1974 and 1979 their friendship grew and blossomed. In that time Cha came to contemplate what a person marrying him would be agreeing to take on. And he couldn't imagine why anyone would welcome such a burden. The situation between Cha and Amanda came to a head over a trip that was planned to India for early 1980 on which Mountbatten would be accompanied by Cha and for which the older man had suggested his granddaughter come along too.

Before the planning could get too detailed it was pointed out to Mountbatten by Amanda's father that if she were to accompany Cha on the trip the press would take it as being as good as an announcement of an engagement. On her return home they would be all over her. And neither she nor the relationship was, as yet, ready for that. If marriage were to come, which was a growing possibility, it should be allowed to do so in its own time. Reluctantly Mountbatten acquiesced to common sense.

In truth Cha and Amanda were not in love. But they

had developed a love, and a respect, for each other. And it was strong enough, on one side at least, for Cha to directly raise the subject of marriage with Amanda. But, apparently, whatever it was that they shared was insufficient for her to submit herself to the sacrifices that such a union would entail. So she turned him down. And Cha, to his credit, could see her point.

Mountbatten, the true Wise Old Man in Cha's life, the man he could always turn to for advice, support, belief and love, the man he had affectionately dubbed 'honorary grandfather', had failed in his grand scheme that would have set Cha on course for all the years to come.

On 27 August 1979, while aboard a fishing boat off Mullaghmore, near the Classiebawn estate he owned in Ireland, Mountbatten was murdered by an IRA bomb.

The evening he heard the news Cha wrote this in his journal:

I have lost someone infinitely special in my life; someone who showed enormous affection, who told me unpleasant things I didn't particularly want to hear, who gave praise where it was due as well as criticism; someone to whom I knew I could confide anything and from whom I would receive the wisest of counsel and advice ... I was lucky enough to have known him for as long as I did ... Life will never be the same now that he has gone ... I only hope I can live up to the expectations he had of me ...

'Don't cry for me ...'

★ ★ ★

IF CHE HAD CHANGED by the time he had arrived back in Buenos Aires, so had Argentina. Barely a week before his return Eva Perón had died of cancer. She was only thirty-three.

Her funeral turned into a carnival of grief and Che had the chance to encounter the phenomenon in full as her body lay in state for two weeks before it was embalmed. To commemorate her a monument was planned that would stand taller than the Statue of Liberty. And though he carried on his work as president, Juan Perón was clearly diminished by the death and mired in mourning.

Che had his own difficulties. The time he had taken off for his journey with Alberto meant he was way behind in his studies. If he was to qualify as a doctor in the current academic year he needed to pass fourteen exams in six months. Things were made even more difficult when on the eve of the first exam he fell seriously ill. He had contracted an infection from working with diseased human tissue in the research laboratory. So worried were his family by his condition that they stayed up the whole night. At six the next morning Che had improved, but he was still clearly ill and physically drained. Despite his father's protests he got up, got dressed and went to sit the exam that began at eight. He passed.

On 11 April 1953 he took and passed his final exam. Leaving the exam hall he found a telephone and called his father:

Doctor Ernesto Guevara de la Serna speaking.

He emphasised the word 'Doctor'.

Almost at once Che planned a new journey. He would travel with an old school friend, Carlos Ferrer, nicknamed 'Calica'. The itinerary they dreamed of was ambitious. First stop was to be Bolivia to see the Inca ruins, then Machu Picchu in Peru, then Venezuela, then Europe, with Paris a particular target. Finally, Che dreamed of making it as far as India.

In the end they never left the continent. But India was not the only destination that Che dreamed of reaching. And his travels with Calica, and especially the political situations he encountered on their way, would bring him closer and closer to his own promised land.

Bolivia was one of the poorest countries in Latin America. Its population was primarily made up of Indians who had been systematically exploited and oppressed. Tin mining dominated the economy. And commercial hierarchies, often foreign controlled, held sway over the mines. But things were changing. A popular revolt had led to the army being disbanded and the mines nationalised. Contentious agrarian reform was next on the agenda. And this was the scenario that greeted Calica and Che on their arrival.

Che wanted to observe the Bolivian revolution at first hand. What he found was a country still in considerable turmoil with different factions within the ruling Movimento Nacionalista Revolucionário jockeying for position. As the people's militia patrolled the streets, and rumours of the disbanded army regrouping to seize back power ran rife, the two travellers fell in, by chance, with the country's social elite.

To contrast the view that their seats at the top tables in La Paz gave them Che went to see the terrible conditions in the mines for himself. At the Bosa Negra wolframite mine they were shown the spot where striking miners and their families had in the past been machine gunned. Now the mine was under the control of the state. And the state was, supposedly, under the control of the people.

On returning to La Paz he was confronted by a scene that revealed that just because a revolution has happened doesn't mean that the people have won. At the Ministry of Peasant Affairs, from where the agrarian reform measures were to be enacted, he encountered groups of native Indians, from different communities, waiting to be seen by the minister in charge. Before entering the building each group was dusted with DDT. The sight outraged Che and highlighted the bitter truth that vast, degrading divides could exist between revolutionary leaderships and the people they were supposed to represent.

The next stop on their travels was Peru and the ancient ruins of Machu Picchu high in the Andes. They found it a place already overrun by American tourists. And it wasn't just the rubber-necking tourists that annoyed Che, as an article he later wrote clearly attests:

> Here comes the sad part. All the ruins were cleared of overgrowth, perfectly studied and described and ... totally robbed of every object that fell into the hands of the researchers, who triumphantly took back to their country more than two hundred boxes containing priceless archaeological treasures ...

The researchers he was alluding to had come from America. If the mines of Bolivia had represented the economic imperialism of the United States, the ancient city of Machu Picchu represented a clear example of the cultural imperialism.

As the travellers headed north the grip that the United States had on the countries they would visit would only be tighter. This was, after all, America's 'backyard'. It is a phrase that reveals the demeaning and patronising way in which the region was regarded.

To Che Central America was a region 'where the countries were not true nations, but private *estancias*'.

They were dominated by dictators and were little better than US-backed banana republics.

El Salvador was run by a coffee-growing oligarchy that naturally depended on exports for any kind of economic success. Honduras was largely undeveloped and was a country almost in service to the needs of the American owned United Fruit Company. Nicaragua was run by the anti-communist General Somoza, who was bolstered in his position of power by the active involvement of US marines used to 'restore order'. And Panama was a state barely fifty years old whose sole purpose seemed to be to give America control over the newly built Panama Canal.

Che's growing willingness to express his developing political views can be seen in the entries he made in his journal after the boat he was travelling on docked in Panama. People he encountered were increasingly described not just in terms of their personality, but also their political 'soundness' too.

From Panama Che travelled to Costa Rica, where he met social reformers and exiled communist leaders. Everywhere he went he observed a world that would only confirm and reinforce the views that had formed within him. And it all led him inexorably towards Guatemala.

Guatemala was a place where a European-descended elite had ruled for centuries. Where the native masses sweated all day on the plantations of the rich, or in the fields of the United Fruit Company. And where, following a reformist 'revolution', a left-wing

Guatemalan colonel, Jacobo Arbenz Guzmán, had just brought in land reforms which ended the power of the elite and nationalized the estates owned by United Fruit.

If there was a front line in Central America in the battle against imperialism Guatemala was it. And that's exactly where Che was heading.

The Cookie Crumbles

☆ ☆ ☆

ON 3 MAY 1979, four months before Mountbatten's murder, Britain had experienced a seismic shock to its system after which nothing would be the same again. It was a shock that had been self-administered. Margaret Brunhilda Thatcher had been elected prime minister. She was the first woman to govern the country since Olivia Cromwell. And before long it became clear that she wore the trousers.

Britain had long been mired in a period of seemingly inevitable decline. On top of that, endless industrial disputes that appeared driven by selfishness rather than solidarity only fuelled the mood of despair. The Labour government of Jim 'Never Had It So Bad' Callaghan may have been in power, but it was clearly not in control. Things came to a particularly festering head during what was subsequently dubbed 'The Winter of the Disco Tent'.

As one strike followed another, and sapped the resolve of a nation that had survived the good old days of the Blitz, municipal workers stopped collecting rubbish and weeks' worth of rotting garbage lined the streets. To the layman the strikes often seemed petty and motivated by greed. But perhaps the straw that finally broke the camel's back was when corpses began to pile up in mortuaries because gravediggers objected to the 'patronising, belittling and degrading depiction of their highly skilled trade' in a production of *Hamlet* that was running at the time at the state-subsidised National Theatre and that dressed them up as clowns. As the leader of the strike put it:

It's all abaht the bleedin' Prince. All abaht his aspirations.
What abaht the aspirations of my members?
When are we gonna get a fair slice of the soliloquies?

And then he added:

Do not, as some ungracious pastors do,
Show me the steep and thorny way to heaven,
Whiles, like a puff'd and reckless libertine,
Himself the primrose path of dalliance treads
And recks not his own rede, mate!

Throw in the fact that the tensions revealed by the Notting Hill Carnival riots of 1976 had continued to simmer and had created enough concerns among the white majority that on their fringes the racist National Front was beginning to gain ground, and it was clear that something had to change. The country, in electoral terms at least, swung to the right.

Mrs Thatcher won an overall majority in the House of Commons of forty-three. On entering 10 Downing Street for the first time she turned to the gathered press and addressed them with the words of St Francis of Assisi:

Where there is discord, may we bring harmony.
Where there is error, may we bring truth.
Where there is doubt, may we bring faith.
Where there is despair, may we bring hope.

As it happens, things didn't really turn out that way.

As she laid into the unions, flogged off the nationalised industries, handbagged the EU, crushed the miners, sold off council houses, Belgranoed the Argies, and presaged a decade in which greed was good, large swathes of Britain were soon quoting from an altogether different religious text. The words in question are those of St Barry of Aussisi and were originally delivered by the Right Reverend Tavares and can be found in the disco-stylee sermon entitled 'More Than A Woman'.

The real problem was that, although there were lots of winners in the new Britain, there were just as many if not more losers. Those who were on the margins became more marginalised. Those who felt that they had little stake in society discovered that not only was what they did have being eroded but, in the words of the Ironing Lady herself, there was no such thing as society.

Unemployment headed towards three million. Social services were slashed. Inner cities erupted into riots as dispossessed youth confronted the police. When the miners went on strike picket lines turned into front lines as the baton-wielding forces of law and order waded in. Harmony, truth, faith and hope were in short supply. Discord, error, doubt and despair seemed to be winning the day.

This is the world that Cha pondered on as he surveyed the start of the 1980s. The royal duty that had been drummed into him since a child meant that he knew he should stay above the fray. But at least he knew that there was a fray to stay above. And while Mrs Tee-Hee saw the mayhem around her as a means to an end, Cha was more concerned that they were the end.

In a country that seemed to worship only the power of the market and the altar of conspicuous consumption, his spiritual concerns were out of step. A world believing that the free market and big business could solve all ills had little time for a man who had read and heeded the warnings of Fritz Schumacher in his seminal social, geopolitical and environmental work *Small Is Beautiful*. For Cha the way ahead was not corporate based but community based. And he saw that the human scale was more important than economies of scale. In a speech he made in America in 1981 he expressed his views like this:

Human beings seem able to endure anything

– except loss of meaning. We need, I think,
to rediscover the importance of the small and
vulnerable as opposed to the materially vast and
physically great. We have to learn that the modern
way of growing great is through growing small
again so that men can operate in small units where
everyone is recognisable as an individual.

Clearly, the man was at odds with the world around him. Not only was he out of step, he wasn't even on the same dancefloor. And as yet very few people paid him any heed. But all fledgling revolutionaries need a time in the wilderness to formulate their views.

In the eyes of the press Cha was still an 'action man': playing polo, hunting foxes, skiing at Klosters and speeding around London behind the wheel of an Aston Martin. But this was also the man who, as early as 1977, had quietly been using his still learning to crawl Prince's Truss as a forum within which members of London's minority communities could meet with senior officers in the Metropolitan Police Force to air their grievances.

How much such meetings actually achieved is debatable. But they clearly show that Cha's concerns were not just intellectual posturings. He may not have been sure what he could do to make things better, but he was sure that he should try. It was all part of what he saw as his duty.

Of course, the other part of his duty was to get married and produce an heir. And, just like in a fairy tale, that's exactly what he did. On 24 February 1981 it was officially announced that Cha, thirty-two, was to marry the nineteen-year-old Lady Diana Spencer. With Britain mired in gloom, societal conflict and upheaval, the prospect of a royal wedding was seized upon as a much longed-for ray of sunshine. Ironically, three decades on from his birth, Cha was once again being used as a fillip for a battered nation.

Cha had first met Diana in 1977. She was the younger sister of his then girlfriend and came across as a jolly, unaffected teenager who liked nothing better than to fashion punk-style dresses out of bin liners and sing along to the songs of X-Ray Specs or the Slits on the radio. She was particularly keen on the latter group's Eurovision Song Contest entry, a radical reworking of The Brotherhood of Man's magnum opus 'Save all Your Kisses for Me'.

Three years later Cha found himself sitting alongside her on a hay bale at a barbecue. He was still profoundly affected by Mountbatten's death. When he mentioned the tragedy she said she had noticed how sad he had looked at the funeral and how she sensed his loneliness and his need for someone to care for him. This touched him greatly. Maybe this was the girl he had been looking for. After all, she ticked so many of the boxes of a potential wife for a future king. The box labelled love remained disturbingly pristine, but Cha's reservations were soon dismissed when he was reminded that this was a *royal* marriage.

As Tina Turner's song written to commemorate the

couple's third wedding anniversary would say, 'What's Love Got To Do With It?'

Anyway, Cha was privately convinced that love, whatever that means, would come in time.

Much has already been written about the story of Cha and Diana, and not just on commemorative porcelain. No doubt much more remains to be. And all of it will be pored over and picked to pieces by the soothsayers and the so-called experts trying to divine the truth. But in the revolutionary kitchen of history the truth is little more than an egg custard that resolutely refuses to set. Dip your spoon below the seemingly solid surface and soon you're scooping your way through mush. Try to grasp it in your hands (never a wise move with an egg custard) and it slips stickily through your fingers.

Little wonder, then, that learned historians and prize-winning journalists have all failed to do the tale of Cha & Di anything like justice. What's more surprising is that a couple of Tin Pan Alley's glitteriest glitterati succeeded in light operatically nailing the custard in question firmly to the mast of public consciousness.

Andrew Lloyd-George and Tim Curry's West End musical *Dianita!* was a smash hit, a cultural phenomenon and a searing indictment of things that needed to be indicted searingly. The show follows the meteoric rise to superstardom and Sky Labic fall to earth of a simple girl from the teeming and poverty-stricken backstreets of Althorpthrop who dared to climb the highest pinnacle of privilege in the land, only to find that the adulation she both craved and generated was but little recompense for the heartache endured. (But obviously the frocks and the Air Miles helped.) And what's more the whole thing was, daringly, done in verse.

The revolutionary flavour of the show can be garnered from its stunning opening sequence:

The curtain rises on a vast deserted stage. For a minute nothing moves. Nothing is heard. Then raised high off the floor on stage left a bedside light is switched on to reveal a woman, mid thirties, hair still tousled from slumber, rising from a double bed in which her husband sleeps on. The woman, wearing an over-sized Garfield T-shirt yawns, stretches, then dons a white candlewick dressing gown. She descends a set of stairs and enters a kitchen. As she turns on the kitchen light, the bedroom light fades.

Sleepily she moves around the kitchen. The remnants of the night before's Indian takeaway are much in evidence. The woman surveys the scene resignedly. Then she spots a bunch of red roses in a glass vase. She sniffs them and smiles to herself. She fills a retro-style whistling kettle and puts it on the hob. As she waits for it to boil she starts tidying the kitchen. The kettle begins to whistle. She puts the takeaway containers in the bin, tips the remnants of a bottle of red wine down the sink and wipes down the worktops with a J-cloth. Then she picks up the vase of flowers. By now the kettle is shrieking. She removes it from the cooker. The almost hysterical noise subsides.

The silence is bliss. She switches on the kitchen radio. A newscaster speaks:

> ... all the authorities are saying at this stage is that a car entered the underpass late last night where it was involved in a collision of some kind and as a result of that incident the Princess of Wales was rushed to the nearest hospital where, in the early hours of this morning, she died –

The woman drops the vase. It shatters. The roses scatter on the floor. The light fades on the kitchen.

From stage right a huge, Mario Testino-style portrait of the radiant, glamorous Dianita slides across until it is centre stage covering up the kitchen. The newscaster enters stage left, giving a brief run-through of Dianita's life. The cleaned-up version. The sanitised one. The one sugar-coated by the PR boil-wash of an early, unexpected death.

The woman reappears. She is now fully dressed. Hair beautifully done. Make-up expertly applied. Clothes elegant, yet glamorous. She clutches the red roses. They are tied with a single white ribbon. She places them in front of the picture of *Dianita*. And looks up.

For the first time the light falls clearly on her face. And the audience sees that her face is the same as the one in the picture. She is Dianita!

A single spotlight hits the bedroom where the action started. The husband stands surveying the scene as if from a balcony.

He is Cha. He starts to sing:

Oh what a sideshow, roll up and stare
The country pulls out its hair
Over the death of a soap star called Dianita
We're acting bonkers
Tears in our eyes, and pain in our heart
How did we end up here
    from such a beautiful start?

That's how to go, to leave the stage
When they've written you out of the script
Demand one last curtain call like Dianita
It's quite an exit
And good for the ratings, a ten out of ten
Britain rules the (air) waves again!

But who is this People's Princess?
Why all this unchecked un-British emotion?
What kind of angel has walked among us?
What will the media do without her?

She'd mastered all the angles, she knew the looks

The best show in town the snappers
outside San Lorenzo shouting 'Di, this way!'
But that's now history
As soon as the grease paint from the funeral
   clears
We'll wake up and see, all along,
   she had fooled us for years

You let us all down, Dianita
Fairy-tale Princess, who should have been
   queen
Was that really too much to ask from
a mixed-up bulimic of barely nineteen?

The show then continues with both Cha and Dianita acting as narrators. Each tells the story from their own point of view. And it is in the gaps between the two competing versions of reality that the audience finally comes to understand the story that it thought it knew so well. And to get to grips with the realisation that often there's a very thin line between fairy tale and tragedy.

Later on, in what is undoubtedly the standout number in the show, Dianita embarks on a gut-wrenching cri de coeur in which an unhealthy relationship with food is but a thinly disguised metaphor for an unhealthy relationship with her husband. Late one night, alone in her kitchen, unsuccessfully in search of something to binge on, Dianita dissects a marriage that has long since turned dry and unappealing. By

the cold light shed by the open fridge door she sings
to the only piece of food she has found – a single slice
of crispbread:

Too dry for me my Ryvita
Eating disorders are just a symptom
A cry for help
From one who has it all
But it's a lonely place
Up on a pedestal

And as for glamour, and as for glitz
I know they get on your tits
They seem a safe haven where I can hide
They are my sanity
Not just the vanity you take them to be
I embrace them while you let me go
I love you and hope you love me

Too dry for me my Ryvita
Eating disorders are just a symptom
A cry for help
From one who has it all
Three in a marriage
Makes my gilded cage too small

The song always received a standing ovation. But
as the run went on young women in the audience
started to get to their feet, not to clap, but to hold
above their heads slices of smuggled-in crispbread that

they would snap in two as a symbol of their empathy with the heroine on stage. At first the theatre management, worried by booming cleaning bills, tried to stop such outpourings of emotion. But unable to rein in the phenomenon they decided to cash in instead. Hence at the interval in the show usherettes offered packets of crispbread for sale alongside the tubs of ice-cream. Of course, the real hardcore fans saw it as symbolic of their complete identification with Dianita to buy both.

The finale of the show was also a deeply moving tableau:

The stage is once again dominated by the portrait of Dianita. In front of it lies the single bunch of red roses. Then Cha walks on carrying a bouquet of white lilies. He places them next to the roses. Then looks up at the picture and starts to sing. He sings 'Oh What a Sideshow' again. But whereas at the start of the evening he sang it with anger, maybe even venom, he now sings it with tenderness.

As he sings people start to appear out of the wings of the theatre each carrying a bunch of flowers. They place them in front of the picture. By the time that the last note of the music has been played and lingers in the auditorium the whole stage is carpeted with flowers.

The picture of Dianita gradually fades. Where the picture was is now revealed as a giant mirror.

The audience is left staring at its own reflection.
And a stage full of flowers.

Guatemala

★ ★ ★

BY TRAVELLING TO GUATEMALA CHE had made a positive decision to be identified with a cause. For a man who had long analysed and thought through the political and social implications of the world he saw round him this move represented a step closer towards a front line. He was no longer satisfied with sitting on the sidelines watching the game. He wanted to be part of a leftist revolution.

As a newly qualified doctor the obvious choice was to apply for a medical post. Arriving in Guatemala he soon met a fellow left-leaning idealist called Hilda Gardea. Eventually she would become his first wife, but when they met her main attractions for Che were her ideas and also the fact that she could introduce him to many of the key players within the revolutionary government.

During the all-night political discussions that Che and Hilda and other radicals often embarked on it soon became clear that Che's stance was far more confrontational than that of those around him. Given the sorry state of Latin American politics he rejected the electoral process. He argued that for a revolution to succeed it would have to bite the bullet and confront 'Yankee imperialism' head on. And he criticised the existing communist parties for drifting away from the mass of the people and being willing to do deals in order to gain even just a little power. For Che the only way ahead was violent revolution.

All the while that Che and his comrades talked the United States government and the CIA – both of which had close ties to United Fruit and were sympathetic to their grievances – plotted to undermine the Guatemalan social revolution. With typical arrogance and bombast they code named their plan Operation Success.*

While waiting to see if he'd be allowed to stay in Guatemala Che watched the developments with growing dismay. In discussions he criticised the Arbenz government as being too complacent in the face of the growing threat from America. With time on his hands, and trying to decide how he could fit into the struggle, he planned a book on the role of the revolutionary doctor in Latin America.

On 26 March 1954 John Foster Dulles – the American Secretary of State (who coincidentally had business links to United Fruit) – managed to get a resolution agreed and signed at a conference of the Organization

---

* Why is it that Americans never name their plans 'Bad Idea' or 'Operation Enduring Imperialism' or 'How the Sam Hill Are We Going to Get out of this One, Bubba'?

of American States that effectively justified intervention in any member state that was 'dominated by communism'. The obvious question that was never answered was who would decide when a state was 'dominated by communism'.

With this diplomatic cover in place, US-backed covert military planning picked up pace in Guatemala's neighbour Nicaragua. Guatemalan exiles were trained. Pilots were hired. Planes smuggled in. Propaganda prepared. And caches of Soviet weapons were stockpiled so that they could be 'discovered' in Guatemala and used to discredit the Arbenz government, so proving that it was 'dominated by communism'.

On 9 April 1954 the CIA (which just happened to be headed by John Foster Dulles' brother Allen – a man with his own links to United Fruit) stepped up the psychological pressure by getting the Catholic Archbishop of Guatemala to issue a pastoral letter that was read from the pulpit of everyone of the country's churches. It denounced communism and called on Guatemalans to rise up. At the same time the CIA dropped propaganda flyers across the country.

On 26 April Eisenhower made a speech to Congress that attacked the Guatemalan government, saying that the Reds were in control. Then he raised the spectre of El Salvador being the next to fall as part of an unstoppable domino effect.

Meanwhile Che was still waiting to acquire his residency. His application dragged on so long, with seemingly so little movement, that he reluctantly reached the decision that maybe it was time for him to move on.

Then on 15 May a ship loaded with arms from Soviet-run Czechoslovakia was discovered en route to Guatemala. It was both the evidence and justification that the US needed to act. And they further racked up the pressure by arguing that the consignment of arms on the ship was clearly larger than Guatemala needed to defend itself and so could only mean that they were planning to attack a neighbouring country. This argument neatly avoided the fact that America itself had long blocked Guatemalan attempts to re-equip its ill-provisioned armed forces and that the only invasion that was being actively planned was the US-backed one from Nicaragua into Guatemala.

Like a skilled conductor the United States orchestrated the rising tension. American warships steamed into the region and stepped up inspections of any vessel bound for Guatemala they deemed suspect. Articles were planted in national newspapers of the region, and propaganda films were shown in cinemas demonising the threat posed by a 'communist' Guatemala.

Arbenz was increasingly backed into a corner by both the covert and explicit campaign co-ordinated around him. Seeking a peaceful way out he tried to negotiate with the US ambassador. His overtures were rebuffed.

By June unease and unrest were so rife within Guatemala that a plot to oust Arbenz came close to succeeding. Even the Guatemalan military that had originally backed him began to waver in their support.

On 14 June, sensing that the country had been softened up enough, Eisenhower decided to bring the situation to a head. He gave approval for the final, critical stages of Operation Success to begin. Two days later American-trained, -financed and -supplied mercenaries began to fly on bombing missions over Guatemala. Two days after that the US-sponsored Liberation Army crossed the border from Nicaragua and invaded the country.

As the first bombs fell on Guatemala City Che admitted to being thrilled by the shock and awe of the violence. In a letter he wrote to his mother he records that 'even light bombings have their grandeur'.

A few days later, as the excitement of the raids was tempered by the grim realities of casualties, he joined up with a medical brigade to help the wounded.

Arbenz tried to play what few cards he had wisely. He allowed the invaders to advance from the border so that any resistance he did put up could not be spun by the Americans as being cross-border attacks, which would allow the 'security' treaties to be invoked. Arbenz also tried to use the UN as a forum to air the reality of what was happening and protested diplomatically to the UN Security Council.

On the ground itself Guatemala's forces were having some success resisting the invaders. The US responded by deploying two more fighter bombers to strafe and bomb key targets. Just how ill equipped Guatemala was to defend itself can be judged from the fact that two more planes could make such a difference. But they did. The tide was turning against Arbenz.

The US also took the fight to the diplomatic front line by frustrating Guatemala's attempts to seek assistance through the United Nations. First they blocked an appeal for a special session of the Security Council. Then they orchestrated a rejection of Guatemala's request that a UN investigative party should visit the country. And when it came to the key votes on the Security Council, America leaned on its allies France and Great Britain, saying that if they didn't support the American side then America would be reluctant to support them in their looming difficulties with Indochina, Suez and Cyprus.

On 25 June the United States won the key Security Council vote 5–4.

Two days later, facing insurmountable odds, Arbenz resigned as the Guatemalan president.

On 3 July Carlos Castillo Armas – the leader of the US-backed rebel forces – flew into Guatemala City in triumph. At his side was the US ambassador. The Guatemalan revolution was over.

As all this had unfolded in the last days of June Che, eager to fight, had joined an armed militia unit. But no sooner had he done this than he was transferred to a hospital unit. Feeling increasingly marginalised in the struggle he talked to whoever in power he could reach and tried to get Arbenz to ignore the wavering military and arm the people. He argued that as the enemy advanced the people could take to the hills and wage a guerrilla war. But it was too late. And he was powerless to do anything except sit and watch the future he believed in collapse all around him.

By mid-July the new regime in Guatemala had embarked on an anti-communist purge. Che knew that it was only a matter of time before they came for him. He made his way to the Argentine embassy and claimed asylum. Within its walled compound he found a varied collection of political refugees all seeking escape from the collapse of a dream that many of them had worked so tirelessly to keep alive.

Outside the walls of the embassy the new government outlawed communism, overturned the agrarian reforms and banned all unions, peasant organisations and political parties. Then they decreed that it was eminently sensible that only the literate be allowed to vote in elections, thus disenfranchising the vast majority of the Guatemalan population.

The US looked on and nodded approval. One part of its backyard had been tidied up.

Che, trapped within the walls of the Argentine embassy, turned down the chance of safe passage to the land of his birth. He had mapped out his future and knew that to get to where he was heading there would be no safe passage.

After a month holed up in the embassy he left and headed for Mexico. In Mexico City he knew he would find a concentration of Latin American nationalists whose views he shared, whose dreams he believed in and who were no longer just willing to sit back and talk and wait for the revolution to come.

It was in Mexico City that Che Guevara, further radicalised and made impatient by his bitter experiences in Guatemala, openly declared himself a communist.

And it was in Mexico City on the seventh of July 1955, almost exactly a year after the failure of the Guatemalan revolution, that the 27-year-old Che met a 28-year-old revolutionary from Cuba called Fidel Castro.

Duty Calls

☆ ☆ ☆

FROM THE OUTSIDE CHA'S MARRIAGE at first seemed to be a great success. Wherever they went they were the golden couple. But as time went on it soon became clear that one half of the golden couple was shining far more brightly than the other. And behind closed doors the differences between the two were starting to reveal themselves. Before long the differences deepened into divides. No doubt both parties were guilty. No doubt both parties were innocent. And no doubt both parties suffered.

Getting married had been part of Cha's duties. And while marriage may have soon become a kind of trap, the very fact of being married had, in part, set him free. That this freedom was to come complete with its own particular set of bars was a circumstance that Cha had not expected.

Of course getting married was only half of the duty he had been contracted to fulfil from the very moment of his birth. The other half was to produce an heir. On 21 June 1982 he and Diana did just that.

William Arthur Philip Louis Limahl Windsor was

born at 9.03 p.m. on that day and tipped the scales at 7lb 5oz. (This included three and a half ounces for the silver spoon in his mouth.)

In a letter he wrote at the time to Mountbatten's daughter Cha said:

> The arrival of our small son has been an astonishing experience and one that has meant more to me than I could ever have imagined.

Reading between the lines of the proud parent's joy you might also just be able to detect the sound of a weight being lifted. He had done the duty that had been expected of him. Maybe it was now time to turn his attention to the duty that he expected of himself.

Guerrilla Warfare

★ ★ ★

FROM VERY EARLY ON in his life Che Guevara was driven by a growing sense of destiny. That some of this sense was self created is without a doubt. But also what is without doubt is that the destiny Che had mapped out for himself came to glorious fruition in Cuba.

On the afternoon of 2 January 1959 Che Guevara drove into the Cuban capital of Havana. A Havana that, in the early hours of the day before, President Fulgencio Batista had flown out of on his way to exile in the Dominican Republic.

Barely two years had passed since Che and Fidel Castro had landed on the island. A few days before they had set sail for Cuba Che had written a poem dedicated to Castro. He gave it to Fidel as the rebels approached the coast.

Let's go, ardent prophet of the dawn
along remote and unmarked paths
to liberate the green caiman you so love …
When the first shot sounds
and in virginal surprise the entire jungle awakens,

there, at your side, serene combatants
you'll have us.
When your voice pours out to the four winds
agrarian reform, justice, bread and liberty,
there at your side, with identical accent,
you'll have us.
And when the end of battle for
the cleansing operation against the tyrant comes,
there at your side, ready for the last battle,
you'll have us ...
And if our path is blocked by iron,
we ask for a shroud of Cuban tears
to cover the guerrilla bones
in transit to American history.
Nothing more.

Eighty-two guerrillas landed in Cuba. After being ambushed by government forces the minute they set foot on Cuban soil only twelve were left to regroup in the Sierra Maestra. In the initial attack Che was wounded and thought himself to be dying. He managed to loose off one shot into the bushes, then lay down and considered the best way to die. The idea came to him that he should be like a character he had read about in a Jack London story called 'To Build A Fire'. In it a man in Alaska, with no wood to light a fire, sat against a tree, mustering what little dignity he could, and waited to freeze to death.

Luckily for Che a comrade, seeing that the wound wasn't fatal, shouted at him to get up and run. Che snapped out of his reverie and did as he was told. As he did so he was faced with a stark choice. In front of him lay a first-aid kit and a box of ammunition. In the retreat to the hills he wouldn't be able to carry both.

He picked up the bullets.

A year after the triumph of the Cuban revolution Che published a book that outlined the theory and the practice of the campaign that he and Fidel had fought. It would become a handbook that revolutionaries the world over would reverentially refer to. Even today. It was called *Guerrilla Warfare*. In its introduction he quoted the French revolutionary Georges Danton's maxim for revolutionary movements: 'Audacity, audacity, audacity'.

What follows are some of the thoughts Che shared in the book:

> Why does the guerrilla fighter fight? We must come to the conclusion that the guerrilla fighter is a social reformer.

> From the very beginning of the struggle he has the intention of destroying an unjust order and therefore an intention, more or less hidden, to replace the old with something new.

> He launches himself against the conditions of the reigning institutions at a particular moment and dedicates himself with all the vigour that circumstances permit to breaking the mould of these institutions.

... very often ... the directors of guerrilla warfare are not men who have bent their backs day after day over the furrow. They are men who understand the necessity for changes in the social treatment accorded peasants, without having suffered in the usual case this bitter treatment in their own persons.

... guerrilla warfare is a war of the masses, a war of the people. The guerrilla band is an armed nucleus, the fighting vanguard of the people.

The fundamental characteristic of a guerrilla band is mobility.

The form of attack of a guerrilla army is also different; starting with surprise and fury, irresistible, it suddenly converts itself into total passivity.

Another fundamental characteristic of the guerrilla soldier is his flexibility, his ability to adapt himself to all circumstances.

... tactics ... should be adjusted continually during the struggle.

At the outset, the essential task of the guerrilla fighter is to keep himself from being destroyed.

As soon as the survival of the guerrilla band has been assured, it should fight; it must constantly go out from its refuge to fight.

When the guerrilla band has reached a respectable power in arms and in number of combatants, it ought to proceed to the formation of new columns.

… it is the countryside that offers the ideal conditions for the fight … the guerrilla fighter is above all an agrarian revolutionary.

The peasant must always be helped technically, economically, morally, and culturally. The guerrilla fighter will be a sort of guiding angel who has fallen into the zone …

Therefore, along with centres for study of present and future zones of operations, intensive popular work must be undertaken to explain the motives of the revolution, its ends, and to spread the incontrovertible truth that victory of the enemy against the people is finally impossible.

Thus, as a product of this interaction between the guerrilla fighter and his people, a progressive radicalisation appears which further accentuates the revolutionary characteristics of the movement and gives it a national scope.

... each one of the guerrilla fighters is ready to die,
not to defend an ideal, but to convert it into reality.

Che's last public communication was a letter he
wrote ten years after the Cuban revolution to an
organisation of international solidarity known as the
Tricontinental. Among other things it was an exploration of the fundamentals of the struggles that still
lay ahead:

We must bear in mind that imperialism is a world
system, the last stage of capitalism – and it must be
defeated in a world confrontation.

The fundamental element of this strategic end
shall be the liberation of all people.

For us, the solution to this question is quite clear:
the present moment may or may not be the
proper one for starting the struggle, but we cannot
harbour any illusions, and we have no right to do
so, that freedom can be obtained without fighting.

We must carry the war into every corner the
enemy happens to carry it: to his home, to his
centres of entertainment; a total war.

What do the dangers or the sacrifices of a man or
of a nation matter, when the destiny of humanity
is at stake?

Wherever death may surprise us, let it be welcome, provided that this, our battle cry, may have reached some receptive ear and another hand may be extended to wield our weapons and other men be ready to intone the funeral dirge with the staccato singing of the machine guns and new battle cries of war and victory.

Another Hand

☆ ☆ ☆

IT IS UNCLEAR WHETHER CHA ever read Che's *Guerrilla Warfare* or, indeed, his letter to the Tricontinental. But whether he read them or not is largely beside the point. That's because by his very actions it would soon become apparent that Cha was an instinctive guerrilla fighter.

He fought and fights because he is a social reformer. He wants to see an end to an order he thinks is unjust. He identifies with the people, but understands that he is not of the people. He recognises that he is the fighting vanguard of the people. And he knows that part of his struggle is to continually educate the people.

When he fights, he hits and runs. He knows that surprise and constant mobility are his strongest weapons. That flexibility must be his watchword. That the countryside is the perfect place to create a base. That agrarian reform is at the core of the revolution. And he knows in his heart that the abstract defence of an ideal is not the point of the struggle, but that the fighter must be willing to sacrifice all in order to convert that ideal into a reality.

Beyond it all he is driven by the belief that the sacrifices of a man matter little when what is at stake is the destiny of humanity.

But there is one area in which, as his own struggle has developed, Cha has stepped away from the framework that Che so charismatically set forth he has widened the definition of imperialism.

Cha Windsera fights against the imperialism of the intellect, of the elites, of the present over the past, of knowledge over wisdom, of scientific rationality and of a worldview that seeks to reduce our very humanity to a mechanistic, materialistic, disconnected state of being.

And he wants to reintroduce mutton to the dining tables of Britain.

What more could any country want from a revolutionary leader?

El Comandante

The First Raid

☆ ☆ ☆

AS WELL AS BEING THE YEAR that Cha's heir was born, 1982 was the 150th anniversary of the foundation of the British Medical Association. In their wisdom they selected Cha to be their president. By rights it should have been a largely honorary role. But Cha had other ideas.

His first speech was made in July. In it he signalled his sympathy with the dispossessed in society by highlighting the problems of access to adequate health care for immigrant groups. He also raised the issue of discrimination faced by the disabled as they tried to lead lives further disadvantaged by society's view of them as a 'problem'.

The speech was well received. And it lulled the BMA into a false sense of security.

The second speech, made in December, was to be an audacious, full-frontal attack on the imperialistic power of the ruling medical hegemony. As Cha addressed the somewhat shell-shocked great and good of the medical profession he clearly stated his belief that the way that they did things was, perhaps, not the only way that things could be done:

> I have often thought that one of the least
> attractive traits of various professional bodies
> and institutions is the deeply ingrained outright
> hostility which they can exhibit towards anything
> unorthodox or unconventional.

He then went on to espouse the possible benefits of a more holistic approach. As his argument was developed he questioned the wisdom of solely seeing 'the body as a machine, and the doctor's task as repair of the machine'.

Then he went on to suggest that,

> By concentrating on smaller and smaller fragments
> of the body, modern medicine perhaps loses sight
> of the patient as a whole human being, and by
> reducing health to mechanical functioning it is
> no longer able to deal with the phenomenon of
> healing.

He questioned why the term 'healer' was viewed with suspicion:

> Through the centuries healing has been practised
> by folk-healers who are guided by traditional
> wisdom that sees illness as a disorder of the whole
> person, involving not only the patient's body, but

his mind, his self-image, his dependence on the physical and social environment, as well as his relation to the cosmos.

Further than this he cited the sixteenth-century physician Paracelsus on the role of the doctor:

Like each plant and metallic remedy, the doctor, too, must have a specific virtue. He must be intimate with nature. He must have the intuition which is necessary to understand the patient, his body, his disease. He must have the 'feel' and the 'touch' which make it possible for him to be in sympathetic communication with the patient's spirits.

And he explained that Paracelsus also believed

that the good doctor's therapeutic success largely depends on his ability to inspire the patient with confidence and to mobilize his will to health.

Finally, Cha laid into the nation's 'frightening dependence on drugs as a universal panacea' and ended up by saying that

the whole edifice of modern medicine, for all its breathtaking successes, is, like the celebrated Tower of Pisa, slightly off balance.

While the assault was full frontal, it was not a total demolition of modern medicine. Cha fully acknowledged that medical science saves millions of lives, and every day alleviates the suffering of millions of people. All he was arguing was that perhaps medical science, with its love of drugs and expensive technology, could be complemented by a more qualitative, holistic, patient-centred approach and maybe have the humility to learn from the wisdom of other traditions, other philosophies and even other spiritual viewpoints.

The speech was not well received.

As Cha finished speaking outraged members of the BMA got to their feet and stormed the stage, hurling their stethoscopes and drug-company catalogues at the podium. As the seething mob started chanting, 'Burn the witch! Burn the witch!' Cha escaped via a side exit.

He had hit. He had run. And now he retreated to his base to plan the next attack.

In the years that lay ahead Cha would return to fight on this front time after time. He would be driven by his sincere belief that 'wisdom has a far more profound meaning than just the acquisition of knowledge in the modern scientific-materialist sense'.

He would argue that 'the meaning that illness has for us is, to a large extent, conditioned by our view about the purpose and goal of the life we are given on this planet'.

He would quote Shakespeare's Macbeth asking a physician of Lady Macbeth,

Canst thou not minister to a mind diseased,
Pluck from the memory a rooted sorrow,
Raze out with written troubles of the brain,
And with some sweet oblivious antidote
Cleanse the stuffed bosom of that perilous stuff
Which weighs upon the heart?

He would reiterate that 'mental and physical health are not simply about medical repairs', and he would argue that, 'We find it hard to accept that there is a need to adapt to loss, and to grieve, and we are intolerant of people who are emotionally distressed.'

Behind it all would be the simple, yet profound, idea that, 'We are not just machines, whatever modern science may claim is the case ...' And despite the ferocity of his initial assault on the modern medical profession he saw his role as one not only of tearing down ivory towers, but also of building bridges:

For well over a decade, I have tried to encourage a more integrated provision of health-care for the ultimate benefit of patients ... we cannot afford to overlook or waste any knowledge, experience or wisdom from different traditions that could be brought to bear in the cause of helping those who suffer.

Also,

Often it seems that complementary medicine

can bring a different perspective and fulfil a real human need for a more personal touch which, in turn, can help unlock the individual's inner resources to aid the healing process. The goal we must work towards is an integrated health-care system in which all knowledge, experience and wisdom accumulated in different ways, at different times and in different cultures is effectively deployed to prevent or alleviate human suffering.

Ever aware that part of a revolutionary's role is to educate, he has set up a Foundation for Integrated Health. And to prove that Cha's concern is not just with high-minded principles, but also with day-to-day practicalities, he has more recently launched attacks highlighting specific problems.

For example in 2002 he raised the growing issue of allergies. He cited a report that 18 million people in Britain have an allergy and that 12 million are suffering from one at any given time. And he went on to state:

In the UK, 34 per cent of thirteen- to fourteen-year-olds now have active asthma, the highest prevalence in the world. I am told that the high figures are most likely explained by lifestyle factors including diet, exercise, smoking in parents, exposure to chemicals and a lack of protective factors in early childhood … and overuse of antibiotics.

El Comandante concluded by suggesting an urgent need to research into the causes of allergies, and of asthma. It is a concern that, strangely, echoed that of an altogether different revolutionary, half a world and half a century away.

The Second Front

☆ ☆ ☆

THE ATTACK ON THE BMA brought a whole range of responses. Obviously those in positions of power, who felt that the very body of their profession was being exhumed and re-examined, fought back. Cha's message was discredited. As was the messenger. But this is always the way with revolutionaries. In the eyes of the authorities all revolutions are misguided and led by fools. However, within a very short space of time Cha found that the banner he had raised was drawing recruits from the massed ranks of the people.

' I have never, ever had so many letters,' he said, adding that 'people often remain silent about what they really think … they are terrified of saying something in case "everyone" should think they are mad'.

Reassured that perhaps the battles that lay ahead of him would not have to be fought alone, El Comandante, following classic guerrilla tactics, opened up a second front.

Barely a year after the raid on the BMA Cha set his sights on the battlefield that Che himself had deemed as being at the core of the revolution – agriculture. The scene was an organic food production conference that was to be held deep in the enemy territory of the Royal Agricultural College in Cirencester. In an introductory message that he had agreed to send he ripped up the anodyne sentiments that had been prepared for him and waded straight into the fray:

> For some years now, modern farming has made tremendous demands on the finite sources of energy which exist on the earth. Maximum production has been the slogan to which we have all adhered. In the last few years there has been an increasing realisation that many modern production methods are not only wasteful but probably also unnecessary ... I am convinced that any steps that can be taken to explore methods of production which make better and more effective use of renewable resources are extremely important. Even if it may be some time before they are commercially acceptable, pioneering work is essential if our planet is to feed the teeming millions of people who will live on it by the twenty-first century.

Read the words now, and they seem hardly radical at all. But just over twenty years ago they were a high-profile assertion of principles that previously were all too easily dismissed as being the namby-pamby, hippy-dippy witterings of the most uninformed of idealists.

But behind the attack was a rigorously thought through analysis.

In Britain much of the problem was deemed to have stemmed from the fallout of the 1947 Agricultural Act. The aim of the Act was, on the face of it, admirable. It sought to ensure that Britain could produce an abundant supply of easily affordable food. What was unforeseen was how such a shift in the emphasis of farming would, in fact, transform the fundamental nature of farming.

As Cha has stated, the system was all about

> economic performance without environmental
> accountability; maximum production without
> consideration of food quality and health;
> intensification without regard for animal welfare;
> specialization without consideration of the
> maintenance of biological and cultural diversity.
> The signals said we wanted cheap food and
> plenty of it ... we can hardly blame our farmers
> now for their outstanding success in achieving
> those goals.

As a result, farmers in Britain's agricultural colleges were trained to think of farming in quasi-industrial terms. The concept that farmers should have the dual role of both producing food and nurturing the land was increasingly ignored. The idea that the soil was a living system in which micro and macro organisms interact with organic materials to produce a complex environment in which plants, animals and humans can thrive was superseded by the view that if you just shovel in enough of the latest fertilizer and additives then everything would be hunky-dory.

All of this meant that Cha was taking a stand against the insidious power of multinational agribusinesses. He championed the cause of ecologically sustainable agriculture that is not in perpetual hock to insistent demands for higher and higher yields achievable only with monocultural superstrains of livestock or plants that demand ever spiralling inputs of bought-in, souped-up nutrients.

He argued that 'the natural world has bounds of balance, order and harmony that set limits to our ambitions'. And that agriculture should be modelled on biology, not on economics.

And he held fast to the concept of farmers as 'stewards' of the land and asserted that,

> Our aim should be nothing less than to restore agriculture to its rightful place as one of the greatest and most important of all the enterprises in which human beings are engaged. Farming, if practised in its fullest sense – and not as another industrial process – is a unique fusion of science, art and culture.

Ever one to lead by example, he ensured that his own Home Farm at Highgrove was managed following organic principles.

But also aware that a true revolutionary must always be vigilant, he has recently focused his guerrilla attacks on the growing menace posed by genetically modified crops.

Cha argues that once released a genetically modified organism cannot be recalled. So the action of the release is irreversible. Also, as genes may spread out into other organisms, the consequences of such a release are inevitably unknown.

He highlights the fact that mankind has

> reached a real moral and ethical watershed,
> beyond which we venture into areas that belong to
> God, and to God alone ... what right do we have
> to experiment, Frankenstein-like, with the very
> stuff of life?

Even for those who feel uncomfortable with his bringing God into the argument, the core of the point is relevant, namely should there be ethical limits on science, or do we just let scientists do whatever they want?

Countering the argument that the production of GM crops is just an extension of traditional plant breeding techniques, Cha states:

> The fundamental difference between traditional
> and genetically modified plant breeding is that,
> in the latter, genetic material from one species
> of plant, bacteria, virus, animal or fish is literally

227

inserted into another species, with which they
could never naturally breed.

And as GM crops are capable of interbreeding with
wild relatives then, 'we simply do not know the long-
term consequences for human health and the wider
environment of releasing plants in this way'.

He also highlights the dangers that inevitably come
with a loss of biodiversity:

Think of the agricultural disasters of the past
which have stemmed from over-reliance on a
single variety of crop, yet this is exactly what
genetic modification will encourage.

But Cha, astutely, also fixes his sights on the capitalist multinational corporations whose profit-driven
imperatives power the industrio-scientific-agribusiness
complexes. For example he points out that, 'most of the
GM plants marketed so far contain genes from bacteria
which make them resistant to a broad spectrum weed-
killer available from the same manufacturer', and that

We are also told that GM techniques will help to
'feed the world'. This is a fundamental concern
to all of us. But will companies controlling these
techniques ever be able to achieve what they
would regard as a sufficient return from selling
their products to the world's poorest people?

And anyway new hybrid seeds that promise higher yields often need fertilizers, pesticides and herbicides in order to thrive. The same companies who create and sell the seeds have monopolistic control of these inputs. What's more, Cha points out, 'the hybrid seed does not breed true, so that the farmer cannot retain seed, but has to purchase every year direct from the supplier'.

Little wonder then that El Comandante can report that

> Representatives of twenty African states, including Ethiopia, have published a statement denying that gene technologies will 'help farmers to produce the food that is needed in the twenty-first century'. [On the contrary they] think it will destroy diversity, the local knowledge and the sustainable agricultural systems ... and undermine our capacity to feed ourselves.

Sixty years ago Che surveyed a landscape in which companies like United Fruit could dominate economies, countries, and the lives of poor farmers. And he fought against it. Today, the names of the companies may have changed, the tactics and technologies may have 'advanced', but the battlefield isn't, in truth, all that different. And Cha, true revolutionary that he is, leads from the front. He fearlessly throws down the gauntlet of resistance:

Do we need to use GM techniques at all? ... Is it not better to examine first what we actually want from agriculture in terms of food supply and security, rural employment, environmental protection and landscape, before we go on to look at the part genetic modifications might perhaps play in achieving those aims?

Once More unto the Breach ...

☆ ☆ ☆

CHA'S NEXT GUERRILLA RAID took on not just the people in the ivory towers, but also the people who built them. What Cha despaired of was that the towers weren't even ivory any longer. They were made of concrete. Or glass. Or the crushed spirits of the down-trodden common man.

On 30 May 1984 El Comandante made a speech at Hampton Court Palace to the Royal Institute of British Architects. It was a speech to mark the 150th anniversary of the Institute's foundation, among other things. Word of its content was leaked to officials of RIBA in advance. Aghast at the attack that they saw coming their way they tried to head off the assault. But Cha was having none of it. He waded straight into the fray, and into an ensuing storm of controversy that is music as sweet to the guerrilla's ears as the sounds of rebel gunfire:

> For far too long, it seems to me, some planners and architects have consistently ignored the feelings and wishes of the mass of ordinary

people in this country. Perhaps, when you think about it, it is hardly surprising as architects tend to have been trained to design buildings from scratch – to tear down and rebuild. Except in Interior Design courses, students are not taught to rehabilitate, nor do they ever meet the ultimate users of buildings in their training – indeed, they can often go through their whole career without doing so. Consequently, a large number of us have developed a feeling that architects tend to design buildings for the approval of fellow architects and critics, not for the tenants.

He then attacked the lack of curves and arches in modern architecture that soften and add feeling to the designs:

> ... why has everything got to be vertical, straight, unbending, only at right angles – and functional?

Quoting Goethe's statement that 'there is nothing more dreadful than imagination without taste', he then trained his guns on redevelopments planned in central London:

> It would be a tragedy if the character and skyline of our capital city were to be further ruined and St Paul's dwarfed by yet another giant glass stump, better suited to downtown Chicago ...

As for the mooted extension to the National Gallery in Trafalgar Square:

Instead of designing an extension to the elegant
façade of the National Gallery which complements
it and continues the concept of columns and
domes, it looks as though we have been presented
with a kind of vast municipal fire station, complete
with the sort of tower that contains the siren. I
would understand better this type of high-tech
approach if you demolished the whole of Trafalgar
Square and started again with a single architect
responsible for the whole layout, but what is
proposed is like a monstrous carbuncle on the face
of a much loved and elegant friend.

But Cha did not only criticise, he also praised. The type of architecture he praised, however, was 'community architecture'. And he highlighted the experience of housing co-operatives where 'the tenants are able to work with an architect of their own, who listens to their comments and ideas, and tries to design the kind of environment they want'.

Also,

What I believe is important about community
architecture is that it has 'shown' ordinary
people that their views are worth having; that
architects and planners do not necessarily have
the monopoly of knowing what is best about taste,

style and planning; that they do not need to be made to feel guilty or ignorant if their natural preference is for the more 'traditional designs' – for a small garden, for arches and porches ...

As you would expect, the vested interests of the self-perpetuating architectural hegemony reacted with fury. Prime among their accusations was the assertion that Cha did not know what he was talking about. Underlying that assault was the thought that he had no right to speak as he did, and that he was abusing his position.

Undeterred, Cha returned to the fray in a speech in 1987.

First he took aim, once again, at redevelopments around St Paul's:

... in spite of all sorts of elaborate rules supposedly designed to protect that great view, your predecessors, as the planners, architects and developers of the City, wrecked the London skyline and desecrated the dome of St Paul's ... they also did their best to lose the great dome in a jostling scrum of office buildings, so mediocre that the only way you ever remember them is by the frustration they induce – like a basketball team standing shoulder to shoulder between you and the *Mona Lisa*.

Then, to rub in the point, conjuring up the ghosts

of Churchill's famous wartime demand during the Blitz that St Paul's had to be saved at all costs, he added,

> You have to give this much to the Luftwaffe: when it knocked down our buildings, it didn't replace them with anything more offensive than rubble. We did that.

As for the competition for leading architectural practices to redevelop Paternoster Square, Cha even laid into the limited horizons of the competition brief itself, which aimed 'to provide as much office space of the highest quality and efficiency, as is possible within the planning constraints' and which called for 'a bold concept for retailing'.

To which Cha commented, 'A bold concept for retailing! What a challenge!', before adding, in reference to St Paul's:

> I suppose Sir Christopher Wren was inspired by the same sort of brief. *Give us a bold concept for worship, Sir Christopher – and the most efficient praying area within the planning constraints.*

He also derided the planning system, stating:

> there must be something wrong with a system which involves public opinion at so late a stage that the only course left open to the public is

to obstruct the development through whatever means the planning system allows.

Years later he was to add that it was all very well for architects to reflect the 'spirit of the age', but where does that get us if the age has no spirit?

In 1988 Cha produced a television programme called *A Vision of Britain* for the BBC that set out his beliefs. Once again thousands upon thousands of the ordinary oppressed masses flocked to stand behind the standard he had raised.

In the book that accompanied the programme he laid out ten key principles for the future. These covered issues of place, architectural hierarchy, scale, harmony, enclosure, materials, decoration, art, signs and lights, and community. And, ever mindful of every revolutionary's duty to educate the very people of which he, as a guerrilla fighter, is only the armed vanguard, in 1990 he set up a Summer School of Civil Architecture. Two years later this evolved into his own Institute of Architecture. And he built the model village of Poundbury in Dorset.

So, once more, El Comandante was waging a classic guerrilla war. Hit and run. Evolve your tactics. Recruit the people. Educate the masses. Assume the moral high ground.

And fight not to defend an ideal, but to convert it into reality.

A Front too Far

☆ ☆ ☆

IN THE MONTHS AND YEARS that followed El Comandante's initial assault on the architectural establishment his ongoing concern with the built environment led him to confront what he saw as another insidious burden that inflicted the people: the state of Britain's inner cities.

Early in 1985 he launched another audacious attack right at the heart of the ruling elite. In a speech to the business power brokers of the Institute of Directors Cha said:

> The desperate plight of the inner-city areas is, I
> am sure, well known to you all, with the cycle of
> economic decline leading to physical deterioration
> and countless social problems. It is only when you
> visit these areas, as I do from time to time, that
> you begin to wonder how it is possible that people
> are able to live in such inhuman conditions ...
> The hopelessness felt in such communities is
> compounded by decay all around, the vandalism
> and the inability to control their own lives in any

way beyond the basic requirements of day-to-day survival in a hostile environment.

The press interpreted his comments as oblique criticism of a succession of governments, including Mrs Thatcher's ruling junta.

In September of that year armed police raided the house of a woman in Brixton whose son was suspected of a firearms offence. The suspect wasn't there, but the police still somehow managed to end up shooting his mother. Brixton erupted into riots of protest and outrage. Though not as widespread as the disturbances of 1981 they carried too many worrying echoes of those events to be ignored. On 1 October rioting broke out again in Liverpool's Toxteth district and in Peckham. Five days later a policeman was murdered during a riot on a housing estate in Tottenham.

All this created a climate of unease in which an associate of El Comandante leaked a story that the press headlined as outing Cha's fears for the future. The biggest fear, apparently, was that we were heading towards a divided Britain of 'haves' and 'have-nots'.

This was a legitimate concern – as Brixton was burning, the City was booming, pushed on by a tidal wave of swilled champagne – but tactically the leaking of the story was a mistake. The press depicted the comments as a direct onslaught on the Thatcher government. This view was further enhanced when the shadow home secretary used the newspaper articles to berate the government in the House of Commons.

It seemed that Cha had stepped away from guerrilla tactics and engaged the enemy in the overtly political sphere where it held all the big guns. And they were big guns that were soon swivelled to face him. In a carefully targeted barrage he was quietly but efficiently hand-bagged by Mrs T.

The message was clear: stick to your own side of the political fence.

What was frustrating for Cha is that he had had no intention of climbing over it in the first place. He was horrified when the story was leaked, knowing full well that any such actions would undermine not only the work he was doing but also the gradual revolution he was trying to bring about.

If he had ever needed proof that the path he must take was that of a guerrilla fighter, here it was in black and white. And blue-rinsed hair.

The turmoil of the times that El Comandante found himself embroiled in during these days was well summed up in the screenplay for the ill-fated movie *Charlie Don't Surf*. Although many have pointed out that the film was a somewhat implausible depiction of events they failed to realise that it was, in fact, nothing but a cinematic version of the magic realism that was, at the time, so in vogue in the world of literature. A magic realism that had its roots in the revolutionary writers of Latin America:

Fade up …

A horizon line of Brixton buildings fills the screen. The air is hazy in early morning sunshine. A thin veil of marijuana smoke drifts up. A distorted slow throb of a helicopter is heard to the left of the screen. The sound of the helicopter gets louder, then the helicopter, so close to the camera that we only see a part of it, sweeps across the frame.

Music: Introduction to 'The End' by The Doors.

Camera starts to pan slowly to the right. Another helicopter, again in close-up, sweeps across the scene.

Music: Jim Morrison starts to sing.

A sheet of fireball explosions engulf the horizon line of buildings.

Thick smoke billows up and obscures most of the screen. Through it we catch only glimpses of fires burning intensely, police helicopters sweeping back and forth, rioters throwing petrol bombs, police shields advancing down a street, cars being overturned or set alight and pushed towards police vans.

Music: Jimbo laments the end of safety and
                surprise and elaborate plans

On the left of the screen an image fades up of an upside-down close-up of Charlie's face. He stares almost blankly out of the screen, clearly lost in thought.

The right of the screen remains filled with a kaleidoscope of scenes of rioters and police, burning buildings and crying children, and the blades of a police helicopter spinning that dissolves into an abandoned police helmet spinning on a road, and finally into a ceiling fan above the bed on which a naked, sweat-soaked Charlie lies.

Music: Mr M desperately seeks out a stranger's hand in a desperate land.

The images of the riots fade. We are left with Charlie on the bed. A voiceover reveals his thoughts.

Charlie (voiceover): Highgrove. Shit. So this was Highgrove. Every time I think I'm going to wake up and find myself back at the Palace. When I was home after my first tour it was worse. I'd wake up and there'd be nothing. I hardly said a word to my wife until I said 'I do' at the altar. When I was away I wanted to be here. When I was here I wanted to be away.

Cut to Charlie as he sits up in his bed. His hand reaches out to a bedside cabinet and he fills a dirty glass from a cherry brandy bottle. He contemplatively knocks back a slug. Rising naked from his bed, he examines his reflection intently in a mirror. He starts the slow motion choreography of Tai Chi.

Charlie (voiceover): I'm thirty-seven now. Still waiting for a mission. Every minute I stayed in the Palace I got softer. Weaker. Each time I looked around the walls move in a little tighter … Everyone gets everything they want. I wanted a mission. And for my sins I got one. No one wanted me to do it. But if I didn't do it, who would? And if I didn't do it, who would I be? Just to wait is no life for a man. Well not for this one.

He smashes his fist into a Louis Quatorze cheval mirror. Then, cradling his bleeding hand, collapses onto the bed and wraps the white sheets around his torso.

Music: Doors track reaches its throbbing climax of thrashing, jangling guitars and visceral drumbeats and young James chanting, Kill … kill …

Charlie pours the rest of the cherry brandy straight down his throat and slides naked and bleeding down the side of the bed, his face contorted with unimaginable existential anguish and pain.

Music: … Kill … Kill … Kill.

A butler appears at Charlie's side.

Butler: Excuse me, sir, but I've laid out your clothes for dinner in your dressing room. And a word of warning: avoid the roulade.

The script then went on to follow Charlie on his mission as he hitched a ride on a 1970s-themed party cruiser that sailed up the Thames into the nihilistic madness that was the City of London in the 1980s. His task was to track down and confront a renegade

Chancellor of the Exchequer who had surrounded himself with his own private army of bare-chested, but still red-braced, amoral city boys permanently out to lunch on champagne, cocaine and obscene bonuses. And who was operating 'beyond the bounds of all decency'.

When he found the Chancellor his mission was to 'terminate his command. With extreme prejudice'. It was to be a soul-searching trip into the very heart of the darkness. As Charlie himself put it as he squatted down in the back of the boat amidst the boxes of silver platform-soled boots, Afro wigs, and six-inch medallions:

Charlie (voiceover): I was going to the worst place in the world and I didn't even know it yet. Weeks away and scores of miles up a river that snaked through the boom years like a mains circuit cable and plugged straight into ... Lawson.

The film's ending was to be as powerful, and probably even more visceral than its opening.

Charlie has tracked the Chancellor down to the Stock Exchange building in the City. At first held captive, late one evening Charlie has now been set free. Lawson, in his own oblique way, knows that he can't go on. And that Charlie must complete his mission.

In the darkness of his office the massive bulk of the bald-headed Chancellor muses on what he has seen and what he has become. On the trading floor his private army indulge in a cocaine-fuelled and Beaujolais nouveau-soaked party that will build to a ritual sacrifice whose significance they are too short-sighted to understand.

As Lawson speaks his face slowly slides in and out of a pool of light, so that we only ever see a small part of him, or a profile of him, or a silhouette. And as his words, uttered with hesitation, but deliberation, and with an elegiac air, drift into the surrounding darkness, Charlie stalks him, armed only with a polo mallet.

Lawson: … you have no right to judge me … It's impossible for words to describe what is necessary, to those who do not know what the Footsie means … the Footsie … the Footsie has a face – and you must make a friend of the Footsie … the Footsie and Unemployment … are your friends … if they are not, then they are enemies to be feared … They are truly enemies … I remember when I became Chancellor … it seems a thousand years ago … we looked at the economy … and we tried to help a country that was ailing … And when we left the Market came … stepped in … and within weeks it had lain waste to our work … all that was left was a pile of P45s and a gust of wind came and even blew those away … I cried … I wept like a

grandmother ... I never want to forget ...
And then I realised ... like I was shot
with a diamond bullet right through my
forehead ... My God ... the Genius of
that ... the will to do that ... Perfect ...
The Market was stronger than me ... than
all of us ... It was run by men ... not by
monsters ... men ... trained cadres ... who
have families ... who have children ...
who are human ... but they have the
strength to do that. You have to have men
who are moral ... but able to exercise their
primordial instincts to trade ... without
feeling ... without passion ... without
thinking. Because it is thinking that
defeats us ...

Music: 'Relax' by Frankie Goes To Hollywood
              kicks off:

The screen cuts to the trading floor of the market. Lit
by the diabolical light of a thousand fat cigars the place
resembles nothing more than the last pit of hell. A bull
is led to the centre of the floor. The head trader, bare-
chested but clad in pinstripe trousers and red braces,
deliberately approaches the bull. The bull's eyes are wide
with terror.

Music: Frankie suggestively suggests that we relax,
              and not do it.

We cut to Charlie as, step by careful step, he closes in
on the seated Lawson who is backlit, in profile, and

dictating into a tape recorder. We hear Charlie's thoughts in a voiceover.

Charlie (voiceover): Everyone wanted me to do it. Him most of all. Even the Market wanted him gone. And that's who he took his orders from anyway.

The music's pounding, hypnotic beat, builds into a frenzy.

Cut to the head trader on the market floor as an associate approaches him with a reverently held golf bag full of clubs. In the feral orange light the trader pulls out a nine iron, then exchanges it for a driver.

Cut to Lawson looking around at the approaching Charlie. In Charlie's hand is the polo mallet.

Cut to the trader raising the golf club above the bull's head.

Cut back to Lawson as he looks away from Charlie and goes back to recording his thoughts.

Cut to the golf club crashing down onto the bull's head. The bull slumps forward.

Cut back to Charlie as he brings his polo mallet down on the head of the figure before him.

Cut back to the trading floor as now all the other City boys, golf clubs in hand, crowd round and rain down blows on the stricken bull.

Music: The music climaxes, then metaphorically reaching for a cigarette fades down.

Cut to the face of a dying Lawson as he lies on the ground. His eyes, opened wide, stare off into the darkness that engulfs him. With his last breath he utters his barely audible final words.

Lawson: … The Footsie … The Footsie …

Fade down.

Credits.

But the film was never made. Financing fell apart when Christopher Biggins passed on the pivotal role of the Chancellor and opted to do a summer season at Skegness instead.

The Path Blocked
by Iron

CHE GUEVARA WAS KILLED as he lay with his hands and legs tied on the dirt floor of a mud-walled schoolhouse on a Bolivian hillside on 9 October 1967. He was emaciated, caked in dirt, with matted hair and dressed in ragged clothes. He did not even have any boots, instead wore on his feet mud-encrusted sheaths of leather.

He had been captured when his dwindling band of revolutionary fighters had been cornered by Bolivian Army Rangers in a small brush-filled gully called Quebrada del Churo. The Rangers had been tipped off about the guerrillas' location by a local peasant.

With the soldiers positioned on either side of the bare ridges of the gully and amply armed with mortars and machine guns as well as rifles, the outcome of any battle was never really in doubt. Che's best hope was to somehow escape. But then a bullet hit, and wrecked, his M-2 carbine. And a second hit him in the calf of his left leg.

He had left for Bolivia a year earlier to lead a revolution there that would have replicated the success that he and Fidel Castro had orchestrated in Cuba eight years previously. In the days and months and years that followed their triumph they had set about rebuilding Cuba along the egalitarian socialist lines that had been the ideal they had both strived towards. It would prove to be as hard a struggle as the guerrilla campaign that had preceded it.

But no matter how difficult it was, Che's pre-eminent role in the revolution meant that, had he wished, he could have lived out his life in Cuba as a lauded and venerated hero. Internationally too his fame and authority were assured in a world in which the struggle against the imperialism of the West, in all its myriad forms, was one of the dominant cultural, social and political imperatives of the day.

Instead, as his letter to the Tricontinental clearly shows, he chose to reject his hard-won position as a general of the revolution and head with a small band of comrades into unknown jungles to create a new front line for the struggle.

Admirable though his idealism was, in many ways, it was a mistake.

Bolivia wasn't Cuba. But the men Che took with him were Cuban. The obvious danger was that they would be seen, and portrayed, as foreign invaders. And this is exactly what happened. Che also fell out with the leader of the Bolivian Communist Party, whose support was vital if unrest was to be stirred in the country's mines and in its capital La Paz. Also working against Che was the fact that Bolivia's previous left-wing regime had instigated a certain level of land reform. Poor though they undoubtedly still were, for the first time in three centuries many Bolivian Indians did own the land from which they tried to scratch a living. The end result was that in the eleven months of his guerrilla campaign in Bolivia Che was unable to recruit a single peasant.

Without the support of the local population there was no chance that his new guerrilla war would succeed.

As the last days of his venture in Bolivia drew to a close it seems as if Che knew that time was running out. Recovered by the Bolivian army when he was captured was a diary that he had been keeping. Somewhere among its final entries is a poem that he wrote for his wife, and that appears to be both a kind of last will and a heart-breakingly tender farewell. It was entitled ' Against Wind and Tide'.

This poem (against wind and tide) will carry my signature.
I give you six sonorous syllables,
a look which always bears (like a wounded bird) tenderness,

An anxiety of lukewarm deep water,
a dark office where the only light is these verses of mine
a very used thimble for your bored nights,
a photograph of our sons.

The most beautiful bullet in this pistol that always accompanies me,
the unerasable memory (always latent and deep) of the children
who, one day, you and I conceived,
and the piece of life that remains for me,

This I give (convinced and happy) to the
  Revolution.
Nothing that can unite us will have greater power.

The morning after Che was captured a Bolivian colonel and a CIA man – ironically a Cuban who had originally been trained by the Americans as part of an anti-Castro brigade – flew in to interview him.

Che refused to be interrogated. But when the CIA man said all he wanted was an exchange of views, he relented. In the ensuing conversation he gave nothing away that would be useful to his captors.

The CIA man busied himself taking photos of Che's diary. Then the Bolivian colonel received orders that his government wanted Che executed. At this point the CIA man intervened and argued that the US government would want him kept alive, at any cost, so that he could be flown out of the country for inter-rogation. The colonel countered that his orders had come direct from the Bolivian president and his joint chiefs-of-staff.

This left the CIA man in a quandary. He had earlier radioed CIA headquarters with news of the capture of Guevara and asked for instructions. But no reply had come back. And the lack of a response sealed Che's fate. The CIA man stepped back from the brink. This was a Bolivian military mission, on Bolivian soil, so the Bolivian military would decide the outcome. And the decision was that Che should die.

Even though this was a decision that the officers

holding Che disagreed with, the order had been given. And at 1.10 p.m., in a mud-walled schoolroom, the order was carried out.

When he was asked if he had a last message for his family Che said,

> Tell Fidel that he will soon see a triumphant
> revolution in America ... And tell my wife to
> remarry and to try to be happy.

Then Che's last words were spoken as a sergeant who had volunteered for the job stepped forward with his gun ready:

> I know you have come to kill me. Shoot, coward,
> you are only going to kill a man.

Che Guevara was thirty-nine.

This I Give to the Revolution

☆ ☆ ☆

AS I WRITE THIS El Comandante Cha Windsera is fifty-eight years old. A year from now he will be fifty-nine. And a year later he will be sixty. And a year on from that he will be sixty-one.

In the almost quarter of a century since he launched his first guerrilla attacks much has changed in the world. And, unfortunately, much has remained the same. What's more, somewhat confusingly, some things have changed while appearing to remain the same. While other things have remained the same while appearing to change.

In a world of such uncertainty is it any wonder that the youth of today cry out for leadership? Cry out for role models? Cry out for heroes?

And while world-weary cynics pour scorn upon anyone who actually believes in anything, it is the youth of today, and of tomorrow (and of the days, months and years to follow) who know that what is all too often derided as 'unrealistic idealism' is in fact realistic unidealism. It is just that it is the product of a different analysis and understanding of our common reality.

Cha Windsera has spent the last twenty-five years (or thereabouts) in a long drawn-out guerrilla war that has this different analysis and understanding of our common reality at its very core. He sees the world not only as it is, but as it could be. And it is a sight that is far from comforting. And while others are content merely to wring their hands and lament the future, El Comandante believes it is his duty to roll up his sleeves, get his hands dirty, and ring the changes necessary to chisel out a future we can all be happy in.

If the notion is fanciful that Cha, the eldest son of such a resolutely privileged and bourgeois family, could become the radical leader of an anti-establishment revolution, and hence the hero that our fractured and disenchanted age needs, so what?

The facts of his life are the testament to his beliefs. And if El Comandante has proved a flawed leader who has struggled as much with the world within himself as with the world without, does this not make him that most valuable of heroes, one who knows himself that he has feet of clay?

To act when you are driven by certainty shows strength. To act when you are riven with doubts shows something, I would contend, more admirable. And much more human.

That he is always at the cutting edge of the struggle that aims for a better world for us all can be judged by brief consideration of the first cause that he ever espoused. A cause that was once considered a minor, peripheral concern to the rich, capitalist, consumerist, egotistical, 'advanced' world of the West. But now a cause that blossoms and flowers like a revolutionary rose, fed with the organic manure of rebellion, in the very heart of the gardens of all men and women of conscience.

The issue was the environment. These days, of course, everyone is on his side. But when Cha first focused on the issue, back in 1970, in one of his earliest public speeches, this was far from the case. Clearly the seeds of his radicalism had been planted early in the soil of his being. Thirty years on those self-same seeds have germinated and grown into a vigorous grove of trees, as can be seen in another speech that he recently gave:

In this technology-driven age it is all too easy
for us to forget that mankind is a part of Nature,
and not apart from it, and that this is why we
should seek to work with the grain of Nature in
everything we do.

And elsewhere he has argued that,

We must, in fact, get back to Nature – not in any
romanticised, drop out, 'under the greenwood
tree' sort of way, but through application of both
science and philosophy.

Also that,

the real challenge, as I see it, is to find the
right blend of dynamic Western systems in all
their purposeful linearity, with the closed-loop
circularity of the natural world. In effect, to
combine modern science with traditional wisdom.

But El Comandante, true man of the people that he
is, is wise enough to realise that top-down, imposed
environmental initiatives, have little chance of success
unless, like a well-planned guerrilla campaign, they
have the grass roots support and understanding of the
people:

Tragically, too many so-called solutions to
environmental problems miss their mark because
they fail to recognise the nature of the societies
which have to put them into effect.

However, he does not underestimate the need for
action. Nor does he shy away from even the biggest,
most powerful of foes. In a 2001 speech in which he
cast his seasoned eye upon the issue of the seemingly
unstoppable, jack-booted, march of globalisation
in its current form, he described the whole concept
as 'deeply flawed and utterly unsustainable'. And in
this phrase he reveals a key tenet of his revolutionary
philosophy – sustainability.

For El Comandante if development is not sustainable, it is, in fact, destruction. And that is something
he will always fight against. And if that means he is

destined to continue his guerrilla struggle, then so be it.

As Cha has continued to wage his intermittent war one concept has grown to become central to all that he does, and to all that he believes. It is the concept of stewardship. And if he could have but one victory in his long struggle, it would be for each and every one of us to accept the concept of stewardship both on a societal and personal level. As El Comandante has stated:

> For me, stewardship operates at two levels; firstly, at the level of good housekeeping … Secondly, it also operates at the level which recognises that we are as much a part of the living world as it is a part of us.

Beyond this Cha believes that the concept of stewardship also means that we, all of us, are guardians of both our environment and our culture, and hence responsible for passing them on to future generations.

Within this visionary analysis perhaps lies the kernel of the nut of the explanation as to just why the future King of England has become the revolutionary radical that so gloriously is El Comandante Cha Windsera.

For all his life, indeed even before he was born, the true historical significance of our beloved leader is not who he is, or what he does, but what he is a part of. And what he is a part of is a long line of ancestors that stretch far behind him in time, and of descendants who disappear way off into the future ahead. In effect, all that he is is the steward of that line. Given that this is an idea that both laced his mother's milk and will no doubt reverberate through the air on the day that he draws his last breath, is it any wonder that the concept of stewardship should be part of his very soul.

Combine this nurturing with Cha Windsera's nature as an individual and the fact that he evolved into a revolutionary leader who so defiantly raises the banner of resistance that proudly proclaims that each and every one of us is a steward of the future is no surprise. In fact, it may even prove to have been a historical inevitability.

The Last Campaign?

☆ ☆ ☆

FIGHTING A RELENTLESS GUERRILLA WAR for so very many years has inevitably begun to take its toll on El Comandante. Look at pictures of him today and the once boyishly tousled mop of hair is grey like the fur of a world-weary badger that is all too used to being periodically baited by the snapping dogs of the tabloid press. His face too bears witness to every heroic struggle that he has endured on behalf of his beleaguered and downtrodden people.

A life of privilege may have its rewards, but a life of duty can extract a heavy price.

But look closer at the self-same pictures and one can't help but see a sparkle in the eye of El Comandante. It is the sparkle of love. And it is a love that is no longer circumscribed by the doubt-tinged qualification, 'Whatever that means'.

It too, however, like so many of the victories Cha has achieved in his relentless campaign, was a hard-won prize wrested free from dictatorial enemies, with vastly superior forces, only after much work, sacrifice and audacity.

The woman that Cha had long loved was Camilla Parker Bowles. But even years after his separation from Diana and her tragic, untimely, death, the prospect of ever being allowed to be seen publicly with Camilla, let alone marry her, was unthinkable. Public opinion, as orchestrated and, apparently, articulated by the media would not stand for it. Even within the royal household of his mother objections were deep rooted.

But El Comandante is nothing if not a fighter. And the prospect of going into battle against insurmountable odds is not one that worries him unduly. After all, why should a man who happily fights the corner of mutton shy away from a struggle to champion the cause of the woman that he loves?

And it is in this last battle, a battle to win the prize closest to his heart, that El Comandante Cha Windsera has revealed his true genius as a master of the strategy, the tactics and the practice of guerrilla war. Because in order to prevail he threw the strategy, the tactics and the practice of guerrilla war out of the window.

The battle in question was codenamed Operation GF. The initials stood for Gladys and Fred, the affectionate nicknames that Cha and Camilla had long used for each other.

Realising that the first step to win over the public to Camilla would involve winning over the media, Cha arranged regular briefings for all the tabloid editors. In particular he focused on the *Mail on Sunday*, the *Daily Mirror* and the *Sun*. This was the first time that

Cha's side had ever been truly proactive with the press, rather than just reactive.

The plan of action that El Comandante had initiated stepped away from his instincts for guerrilla raids in as much as it was a subtle, long game, and one devised to succeed almost surreptitiously. Gone were the audacious attacks of old. In their place Cha acted like a seasoned hunter, quietly stalking his prey.

El Comandante also realised that even within the institution he would one day lead, hearts and minds had to be won over. Once again he and his small cadre of comrades trod softly. Camilla was allowed to sit in on the vital diary meetings that considered and decided just what events would be included in his always busy schedule months or even years in advance. It soon became apparent in these sessions that she both understood and supported all that he was trying to do. Gradually respect for her opinions, her involvement and indeed herself grew.

Next a meeting was quietly 'arranged' between herself and Cha's sons. And news of the meeting was 'leaked' to a press that was slowly becoming more sympathetic.

Not long after this Camilla played host at Highgrove at a party to mark Cha's fiftieth birthday. Three hundred and forty-two guests attended, including Cha's sons and other members of the royal family. The queen, however, still would not agree to meet her son's new partner.

As each step in the campaign was taken the public

response was carefully monitored to see if a backlash would come. But it never did. Of course there would always be those who would never accept Camilla. But as time went on their significance began to fade.

In 1999 the couple were photographed together for the first time leaving an event whose location was once again 'leaked' to the press well in advance. Then Camilla started to attend official court occasions. Even though she was still to meet the queen, this clearly indicated that Her Majesty was coming round.

By now Camilla's appearance had been 'updated'. The transformation had been effected by the TV royalty of makeover gurus Grinny and Havana. Over cups of Camp coffee perked up with G&T chasers the television experts revamped and revitalised Camilla's look and were odds-on for MBEs or even damehoods when, whilst Havana danced her trademark salsa, Grinny made the mistake of grabbing Camilla's boobs to illustrate some point that could easily have been illustrated without boob-grabbing but would not have made anywhere near as good TV. Despite this etiquettal faux pas the makeover itself was a considerable success. Camilla would never be loved by the camera as her predecessor had been, but now at least the camera and Camilla were on reasonable nodding acquaintance terms.

Operation GF continued with Camilla's first appearance within Buckingham Palace at an official event, then a family holiday aboard a yacht, and after that a solo tour of America.

Cha was heartened to see that it was a campaign that was bearing fruit. And in June 2000 the top banana of the fruit that it was bearing fell, finally, into his lap. His mother agreed to meet Camilla. The occasion was a party being held at Highgrove to mark the sixtieth birthday of King Constantine, the ex-ruler of Greece. The meeting lasted less than a minute, during which Camilla curtseyed and the queen, betraying her wicked if rarely revealed sense of humour, asked her favourite question 'And what do you do?'

A year on from this momentous occasion the tabloids got the photo they had longed for when, at a party to mark the fiftieth anniversary of the National Osteoporosis Society of which Camilla is the president, Cha kissed her on the cheek. The picture was relayed around the world. For the next five years Operation GF continued with such success that on 9 April 2005 El Comandante Cha Windsera and Camilla Parker Bowles were married.

If the wedding was not greeted with the national rejoicings of his first union it was entirely understandable. But on the whole most people wished them well. Which, after all, is a far more realistic response.

However, emboldened by the success of the wedding, and having, temporarily at least, won over the tabloids, Cha reverted to his guerrilla instincts and decided to launch one last audacious attack right at the heart of the media intelligentsia that periodically sneered at his every move.

He arranged for his wife to give her first ever in-depth interview on BBC2's *Newsnight* programme. And in a truly daring twist he hoped to highlight the seriousness and dedication of his partner's work for the National Osteoporosis Society by having her interviewed by the pit bull of politics himself, Jeremy Paxman.

The interview, which would turn into a broadcasting legend, was to be the first time that most of the nation would ever hear Camilla speak.

Unfortunately it didn't quite go the way that El Comandante had expected. What follows is the full, unexpurgated transcript of the interview. And it can be seen that right from the start Paxman, ever mindful of his own image, veered off the agreed line of questioning.

Paxman: In a first for *Newsnight* I'd like to welcome ... the Duchess of Cornwall.

Camilla breaks off from texting on her mobile and looks up at Paxman.

Camilla: Innit.

Paxman: It must be strange being called 'Duchess'?

Camilla: Innit though.

Paxman: What's it like being royalty?

Camilla: Arright.

Paxman: Yes, but what's it really like?

Camilla:	Arright.
Paxman:	What about the perks?
Camilla:	It's arright, mate.
Paxman:	What about the clothes, who pays for those?
Camilla:	Are you callin' me a Pikey?
Paxman:	No, I'm –
Camilla:	Are you callin' me a Pikey?
Paxman:	No, I'm jus–
Camilla:	Coz I'm not even a Pikey.
Paxman:	No, I was just raising –
Camilla:	Are you disrespectin' my family?
Paxman:	I'm –
Camilla:	Are you disrespectin' my family?
Paxman:	I didn't even mention your family.
Camilla:	Are you ignorin' my family?
Paxman:	No, I'm –
Camilla:	You're ignorin' my family.
Paxman:	I'm not ignoring your family.
Camilla:	You're pickin' on my family? You wanna leave 'em alone. What they ever done to you?

Paxman changes tack.

Paxman: What was the wedding like?

Camilla: It was well good.

Paxman: Well good?

Camilla: Wicked.

Paxman: Wicked?

Camilla: Mash-up.

Paxman: Mash-up?

Camilla: Innit.

Paxman: It was enjoyable?

Camilla: Innit, though.

Paxman: Did the public purse pay for the enjoyment?

Camilla: Are you callin' my dad poor?

Paxman: No, I'm –

Camilla: Are you callin' my dad poor?

Paxman: No, I'm just –

Camilla: Are you saying he got his suit from Matalan?

Paxman: No, but –

Camilla: It didn't even come from Matalan.

Paxman: I didn't –

Camilla: But it didn't even come from Matalan though.

Paxman: No, I'm just –

Camilla: Are you disrespectin' my dad's suit?

Paxman: No –

Camilla: Coz I don't need it.

Paxman: I'm just –

Camilla: I don't need it.

Paxman: I'm –

Camilla: I just don't need it, mate.

Paxman: If you just let me get a question –

Camilla: Do I care?

Paxman: … a question about the legitimate matter –

Camilla: Do I care though?

Paxman: … of the cost of –

Camilla: But I don't care, mate.

At this point Paxman completely loses it and goes for the jugular.

Paxman: You know you'll never be queen.

There is a long pause as Camilla looks Paxman up and down. Then looks away.

Camilla: Am I bovvered?

Paxman: Never wear the crown.

Camilla: Am I bovvered?

Paxman: Never be called 'Her Majesty'.

Camilla: Am I bovvered though?

Paxman: Never appear on stamps.

Camilla: I'm not bovvered.

Paxman: Or on coins.

Camilla: Do I look bovvered?

Paxman: Never –

Camilla: Does my face look bovvered?

Paxman: … ever –

Camilla: Is this face bovvered?

Paxman: … ever –

Camilla: Face?

Paxman: … be –

Camilla: Bovvered?

Paxman: … the –

Camilla: Face?

Paxman: … queen.

Camilla: Bovvered?

Paxman: You'll always just be the plain old Duchess of Cornwall who most of the country, including your new father-in-law, can't understand why your husband preferred over his beautiful and glamorous and publicly loved first wife.

Camilla: I. Am. Not. BOVVERED!

At this point the interview was ended by the duchess's press secretary and she was ushered away. Then later that evening as she was waiting outside the studio she got into a fight with Newsnight's *political editor Martha Kearney as to whose car had turned up first.*

For Cha and the team who had orchestrated Operation GF the interview had turned into a disaster. All the hard work of the preceding years had gone up in smoke. Desperately they tried to have the interview pulled. But, even though Paxman had veered away from the innocuous questions about Camilla's charity work that had been supposed to comprise the bulk of the interview and headed into more contentious territory the BBC, citing their Charter remit to 'serve the public', insisted on broadcasting the interview in full.

The result was as remarkable as it was unexpected.

The British public took Camilla to their hearts. She had gone into the lion's den of media examination that even the likes of Tony Blair shy away from, and come out, if not with a resounding victory, at least ahead on points.

The tabloid headlines the day after the broadcast summed up the national mood. The *Mirror* ran with 'Camilla Parker-Not-Bovvered'. The *Mail* had 'The Duchess of Duke It Out Street'. And the *Sun*, in a fleeting reference to a disparaging nickname once applied to the duchess, ran the following headline over a picture of Camilla standing with one foot resting on the prone body of Jeremy Paxman:

Pit Bull 0 Rottweiler 1

El Comandante having seemingly snatched defeat from the jaws of victory had somehow managed to stand on the beach of public opinion and get the incoming tide of media disdain to turn back.

At last he could face the future with the woman he loved by his side.

The Future

☆ ☆ ☆

IT IS ALMOST a quarter of a century since El Comandante Cha Windsera launched his first guerrilla attack. In that time he has taken the fight to many new fronts. And confronted many new foes. There have been successes. And there have been setbacks. And personally, too, El Comandante has been through the fire. But he has come out the other side.

He has been vilified, ridiculed, lambasted, declared unfashionable, derided as irrelevant, decried as naive and denounced as a hypocrite.

Yet still he fights.

Whether he's trying to save the environment, or highlight the plight of the wandering albatross, he wades fearlessly into the fray. Though the odds are against him. Though the chances of victory are slim. Though he knows that the sniper fire of ridicule will always have him in its sights.

Yet still he fights.

He has sought meaning in a meaningless world. He has searched for purpose in a purposeless life. And he has looked within himself and doubted all that he has seen.

Yet still he fights.

But now El Comandante needs us at his side. Because his end draws near. And it will come not in a hail of bullets, but in a fanfare of trumpets. Because before they can lower the crown onto his head they will have to remove the beret from it.

Then it will be up to us, up to all of us, to continue the fight. Which is only just, as it is after all, our fight that he has been fighting.

Viva Cha!

Acknowledgements

THIS BOOK IS, to a very large extent, absurd. But perhaps the most absurd thing is that a surprisingly large proportion of the information it contains is true. Most of this information comes from sources that are far better written and more meticulously researched than this one.

My primary source for Prince Charles was Jonathan Dimbleby's *The Prince of Wales*, which I used as the basis for the prince's life story and which also provided many of his quotes. The material on his speeches towards the end of the book draws from David Lorimer's *Radical Prince: The Practical Vision of the Prince of Wales*.

Che Guevara's biographical details are from Jon Lee Anderson's excellent *Che Guevera: A Revolutionary Life*. If you are at all interested in Che I recommend it highly. It's 800 pages long but, like Dimbleby's book on Prince Charles, a real page turner.

Of the source material drawn on for the parodies in the book, I would like to acknowledge the unique place in comedic history of Spike Milligan et al.'s 1950s *Goon Show* scripts, which are as funny and as strange today as they were half a century ago, and, at the other end of the temporal spectrum, the superb Catherine Tate, whose character Lauren I have misappropriated unashamedly for the Camilla who faces down Jeremy Paxman on *Newsnight*. And of course Charlie Don't Surf is a spoof of the epic *Apocalypse Now* written by John Milius and Francis Ford Coppola, while Dianita is a warped version of Andrew Lloyd Webber and Tim Rice's *Evita*.

Other stuff in the book I just made up. It seemed the most appropriate way to write about Prince Charles.

Bibliography

Marianne Alexandre (ed.), *Viva Che! Contributions in tribute to Ernesto Che Guevara* (Lorimer Publishing, 1968)

Jon Lee Anderson, *Che Guevara: A Revolutionary Life* (Bantam Books, 1997)

Vernon Bognador, *The Monarchy and the Constitution* (Clarendon Press, 1995)

Gyles Brandreth, *Charles & Camilla: Portrait of a Love Affair* (Century, 2005)

HRH Charles, Prince of Wales, *The Old Man of Lochnagar*, illustrated by Sir Hugh Casson (Hamish Hamilton, 1980)

— *A Vision of Britain: A Personal View of Architecture* (Doubleday, 1989)

HRH Charles, Prince of Wales and Charles Clover, *Highgrove: Portrait of an Estate* (Chapmans, 1993)

Jonathan Dimbleby, *The Prince of Wales* (Warner Books, 1994)

Caroline Graham and John Blake, *Camilla and Charles: The Love Story* (John Blake, 2005)

Che Guevara, *Bolivian Diary* (Pimlico, 2004)

— *Guerilla Warfare* (Souvenir Press, 1961)

— *The Motorcycle Diaries* (HarperPerennial, 2003)

— *Reminiscences of the Cuban Revolutionary War*, new edn (Ocean Press, 2005)

Penny Junor, *Charles: Victim or Villain?* (HarperCollins, 1999)

David Lorimer, *Radical Prince: The Practical Vision of the Prince of Wales* (Floris Books, 2003)

Spike Milligan, *The Goon Show Scripts* (Woburn Press, 1972)

— *More Goon Show Scripts* (Woburn Press, 1973)

Andrew Sinclair, *Che Guevara* (Sutton Publishing, 1998)